NEPTUNE'S
daughter

journey into oneness

NEPTUNE'S
daughter

journey into oneness

Julie Yau

mystic-Hill publishing
Laguna Beach

Published by mystic-Hill publishing
Laguna Beach, California
E-mail: julie@julieyau.com
Author's Website: www.julieyau.com

ISBN: 0-9740324-0-9
Library of Congress Control Number: 2003092570

Cover Design & Photograph by Chris Varosy
Page Design by Janice M. Phelps

PRINTED IN THE UNITED STATES OF AMERICA

Contents

Acknowledgments

To all of those who encouraged me to share what is infinitely personal, I am so grateful.

To my "rebels with a cause" team: David Courtemarche, Sarah Johnsen and Nancy Burcham, whose support was so important in the creation of this project. And to Nancy again for your wonderful insights.

Great thanks to Nancy Greystone for your great encouragement and help in editing.

I am grateful to my husband, Sam Yau. Thank you for all your love, friendship, support and for believing in my journey.

To all my teachers, I am forever indebted.

Preface

I wrote and performed a monologue a couple of years ago, for a personal growth workshop at the Esalen Institute in Big Sur, California. It was a monologue about the extraordinary phenomenon and rather strange experiences of my life. I called it "I Have a Peculiar Gift." I put on a thick Irish accent, and quite humorously portrayed a middle-aged Irish woman explaining, in her way, what it is like to see beyond our ordinary reality. It was not my objective to be believed, even though everything I spoke was the truth, but to explore my own being. These were incidents that I had kept to myself — reverent, spiritual and often indescribable. At the time of this particular workshop I felt ready to discover more of who I am, which I realized included my ability to see and experience beyond what we think of as ordinary reality. I loved how the universe supported me as I courageously stepped forward to do this.

I was utterly delighted with the response. As my performance came to a close with the words, "Ay, it's a peculiar gift." I gave a little bow, and to my astonishment every one stood up and applauded.

The depth from which I spoke resonated with everyone, even with the humor. Some had tears in their eyes and some were deep in thought about the revelations. I was touched and humbled by their response and encouraged to share more. Their interest and enthusiasm became the catalyst for this book.

Writing this book reveals some of my most intimate experiences. I believe they reach far beyond my personal self to a consciousness that touches all of us. I felt excited and apprehensive at the prospect of revealing my stories, and it became an enriching creative adventure for me.

The essence is about consciousness and awareness. It is about mystery and epiphanies, and it is about the infinite possibilities that await all of us. Essentially it is a journey into union with the Divine, a journey to Oneness.

I see the afterlife, and have had strange and horrifying meetings with bizarre creatures. I have come face-to-face with ghosts and entities. I have encountered strange beings, flown out of my body, realized the truth of the inner journey, been held by angels, experienced the terrifying depth of my own feeling of separation, and experienced the phenomenon of human consciousness in its separation, pain and healing.

In my late twenties these unusual events happened often. Every two weeks or so something peculiar occurred, a little earthquake to shake up my reality. An expansion of awareness would take place, challenging me to look at life with a new perspective. I realized there was a greater purpose — something incredibly significant was happening to me. It was difficult to understand my psyche with intellect alone. I recognized that the mysteries of the universe are so immense, vast and poetic, that trying to conceptually understand and analyze them all was too much, and so I surrendered to the mystery itself.

My yielding to the winds of existence has brought a deeper understanding as I continue to absorb myself in ancient teachings and new insights as I continually stay open to the wonders of life. Beyond the illusion, there exists only one reality; there is a beautiful orchestration of divine existence possible for us to explore — it is that which we are.

If I happened upon difficulties while writing, it was with language. I found a certain level of frustration as I tried to articulate events that were so often ethereal, words were barely adequate to describe them. However, language is one of our greatest gifts. I was conscientious in my attempts to convey my experiences sincerely and articulately. I enjoyed navigating my way through the experiences with words. When I draw upon expressions like "bliss," "ecstasy," "oneness" and "unconditional love," they are not used superficially, but are intended to express their deepest sense. I also found it necessary to occasionally impart a certain level of lightheartedness. There is an immense amount of humor in the universe, and laughter truly is a great medicine.

In my early twenties and with a significant shift occurring in my conscious awareness, I began to study the transpersonal realms of psychology. These choices of study became a transition point into a deeper understanding of my own psyche. This allowed me to cultivate an ability to move profoundly into my own unconscious, what Jung called the collective unconscious, and beyond. I found a framework for some of the unusual experiences I had encountered earlier in life, and a strong vessel to hold profound spiritual experiences that were to come.

I had no idea how deeply affected and how intensely gratifying studying psychology, the human body and consciousness would be. My enthusiasm for knowledge grew and for the next ten years my awareness expanded as I traveled this stimulating and exhilarating path. I studied many techniques which incorporated deep process work, where I rediscovered my essential connection to the universe. I found a community that accepted me unfalteringly. My unique and unusual encounters were received without question, and recognized as extremely healing and insightful. I was able to embrace and nourish my experiences, knowing I was not alone in having these rather strange encounters.

Everyone's journey is, of course, different, and there is more to be experienced than ever can be told. I believe there is a new paradigm emerging, of self-discovery and self-healing for all of humanity. We all bear a burden at some level. I believe this is connected to an intricate webbing of pain beyond the personal and beyond time. It is possible while healing ourselves that we are easing the collective pain. We tap into a larger identity and so our therapeutic resolve and learning far transcends our personal self. We are all part of what Jung called the *anima mundi,* or world soul. There was no question in my mind, after a few of my experiences, that I went far beyond my own identity and entered into a field of awareness that transcended our time/space. As you will see in later chapters, I experienced a profound collective suffering, which I believed to be deeply healing for that particular field of consciousness. Interconnected and all part of a whole, when we put into action our personal healing, it does reach far beyond the self.

For more than half a century now, we have witnessed an emergence of desire for self-healing through experiential therapies. There are numerous therapies, from Holotropic Breathwork, to Ecstatic Dance to Emotional Release Bodywork that can help induce non-ordinary states leading to amazing self-healing and transformation. There is an empirical interest in consciousness and spirituality characterizing an exciting period in time for all of us. An enthusiasm for the study and practice of shamanism is gaining popularity. People are traveling around the world to experience healing and transformation with indigenous shamans, searching for meaning and growth. I have met many people from all walks of life who are incorporating shamanistic practices and ritual into their lives. Successful business people, professionals, artists, and students are going on retreat to journey with Ayahuasca, a Peruvian mixture of plants that induces altered states of consciousness. There are numerous books lining the shelves on Shamanism, and workshops are plentiful to learn the ritualistic inner journeying and self-discovery techniques. Spiritual philosophies of the East and mysticism of all countries are becoming more commonplace in conversations, reflecting the spirit of the time. We are looking beyond the ordinary and embracing ancient wisdom, to find answers for wounds, addictions, internal conflicts, cultural enmeshment and a deeper meaning to life. I believe what I have and continue to encounter is becoming more widespread and the stories are emerging in abundance as we unravel ourselves from our limited interpretations of reality.

I am continually grateful for my ability to transcend the ordinary spontaneously or with little effort, as sometimes the world felt so full of meaningless suffering. There had been times in my life I felt so sad, unsure how I would go on; but my enduring spirit, touched by all the magical and spiritual encounters, as well as seeing the awesomeness of everyday existence, continued to encourage and inspire me to heal and to live. I found out I was never alone; separation is an illusion. That is the message I want to convey to everyone. We are all connected and we can all experience this awesome revelation to the extent that it can help us in our lives here and now. When our separate sense of self loses its power over us, we can claim back our knowledge of who we truly are and live life to its fullest.

My title, *Neptune's Daughter*, came to me after studying archetypes. Jung thought of archetypes as the basic constituents of the human psyche, and viewed them as universal expressions of a collective unconscious. James Hillman regarded archetypes as Gods of the psyche. Caroline Myss believes archetypes are the architects of our lives, through which we can better comprehend ourselves. With my ability to see beyond the "normal," and a certain faculty to experience the numinous and paranormal realms, I was curious to see which archetypal influences prevail in my life. The spiritual seeker with spiritual sensitivities and permeable boundaries, that of the planet Neptune, I discovered, is a very strong influence. This Neptunian energy has been very influential in my life, with positive and negative attributes. Neptune is the archetype of the transcendent, of the spiritual, associated with dreams and visions, magic and beauty. It symbolizes the ocean of consciousness that dissolves all boundaries between self, other, the universe and God. As vessels of awareness, we are not estranged from the universe as a whole, but an extension of it. The goal of most spiritual seekers and all religions is essentially a Neptunian one: union with the Divine. As you continue to read you will recognize and come to see how applicable this has been for me.

With a strong existing connection to a Universal God from a very young age, I did not undergo any major conceptual adjustments or drastic revisions of my beliefs as unusual encounters unfolded in my life. As a child I knew "God" was not a personal entity, but an ever-present energy of love and acceptance. I was connected to the mysterious; the dancing energy of auras filled my child's eyes with delight that captivated me. Butterflies and bees, mountains and grass, starfish and sand were all enchanting parts of a magical world that I watched with innocent eyes. I could feel what others felt, I was receptive to energies of the earth, and I welcomed the presence of Mother Nature as I allowed my boundaries to merge. I realized soon that this was not "normal" and tried to shut off my openness. As I grew up and entered, experientially, the transpersonal realms, I once again allowed myself access; there was no desire to turn back. My world became intimately interwoven with other realms — the mystery too alluring, too striking and too remarkably authentic to turn away from. My experiences and encounters touched me too deeply and compassionately in my heart and soul, to not want to continue to explore.

The unpredictable and exciting adventures that have thrust me into riveting moments of wonder and enchantment as well as the mysterious, and the sometimes frightening, have brought myriad emotions. From joy to sadness, there has always been an underlying feeling of connection and peace, and of course an inexorable curiosity. I feel drawn to share these experiences; I feel in my heart I am offering a gift in return for the wonderful ones I have received.

As I integrate the spiritual events into my daily life, my world becomes enriched with divine illumination, meaning and an inspiring depth. I am encouraged to fulfill all that I am, while I am here. I am far more able to stay in my heart, to feel compassion at the most painful times and refrain from judgment and anger. I work to be present and empathetic, knowing I am a soul on a journey of human experience and part of a brilliant tapestry of unimaginable levels of consciousness in an extraordinary universe. I found a universal consciousness that is a continuum of creating motion. We are unique expressions of this creation, infinite and absolute. What I have witnessed are the mysteries of life from a beautiful place of belonging. We are continuously catapulting ourselves into ever-new expression, and ultimately what I found is that the greatest joy is that of Spirit to experience itself through us, as us.

My sense is it is time for us to move from apathy to exploration in order to be a part of the transformation of the world in which we live. Part of what we can do is to restore tranquility and equilibrium within ourselves. If everyone does this, there will undoubtedly be peace, and a wonderful continuation of the evolution of consciousness.

Cosmic Dance

My body twisted and contorted; I was moved as if I were a rag doll. I was aware I was moving into yoga positions I could have only dreamt about. Later I understood where yoga, meaning union, origi-nated, and the purpose of the practice. My personal practice would profoundly change. Yet I had not been practicing yoga postures, but had been sitting in vibrant stillness and meditation observing my breath quietly move through me in gentle waves, when by some unex-pected force, I was propelled into a non-ordinary state and a journey of self-realization. There was a great emergence of energy that moved my body like a snake. Impulsively opening the energy pathways and centers, allowing and demanding absolute freedom of movement, the energy delightfully spiraled upward. It was not my brain or my thinking mind that moved me, but pure cosmic energy, purging and purifying my body, tossing and turning me, stretching and shaking me to my core until one final thrust threw me from the wheel position onto my belly. With my chest, neck, arms and legs reaching backward and upward toward the sky, fervent power streamed unmercifully yet gloriously through me. In the dynamic stillness of the intense position my breathing was heavy and heartbeat racing. Great cosmic bubbles of joy and excitement began to well up in my lower belly. I could hear dramatic moans coming from me as the awesome feeling grew and multiplied. The brilliant bubbles turned to rapture and moved exhila-ratingly upward exploding spectacularly in the region of my heart. I was thrust wildly into a huge cosmic orgasm. Over and over again the bubbles exploded, filling every cell of my being with ecstasy and euphoria. Finally any notion of a separate Self disappeared, shattered by bliss and divine luminosity and there was only Oneness. One Spirit realizing itself in exquisite indescribable love of a magnitude unbeknownst but to those who awaken to its glory. One, and that is all.

– Arizona, May 2002

Chapter One

Seeing is Knowing

We are not human beings having a spiritual experience.
We are spiritual beings having a human experience.
–Teilhard de Chardin

I WAS ON MY WAY TO VIRGINIA, to the foothills of the Blue
Ridge Mountains. I felt an inner charge of excitement
knowing I was on a journey of self-exploration. The Blue
Ridge Mountains have always conjured up images of mystery
and unexplored beauty for me. Growing up in England, I loved
the exoticness of the name of this place in a far-off land.
Fourteen years after my initial move to California, I was on my
way to the foothills of these splendid mountains, yet not for any
reason that I would have imagined in my younger years. I was
going to Virginia to attend the Monroe Institute to learn more
about consciousness, and nothing could have quite prepared me
for the extent of the insight and perception I received. The week
was profound, enlightening and intrinsically mysterious.
Through a bona fide experience beyond the boundaries of our
physical reality, my knowing of the world changed forever.

In the course of these explorations I found myself in realms
and dimensions that I had not previously thought existed. In
natural meditative states, I wandered through belief systems
created by our own minds. Heavens, hells and much in
between; spectacular matrices of reality that people go to after

death. It is interesting how later I learned of the various worlds of Tibetan Buddhism. A three-fold division of Heaven, Earth and Hell, which are subdivided into six realms. These realms contain: the god realm, the jealous god realm, the human realm, the animal realm, the hungry ghost realm and the hell realm. These realms correspond to six psychological states: bliss, jealousy/lust, passion/desire, ignorance, poverty/possessiveness, and aggression/hatred. Realms that not only exist after death, but states that can be recognized in our everyday living, which keep us bound to our limiting beliefs. Through my experiences I learned that after dying you go to where you expected you might. I saw people stuck in their desires and ignorance, as well as their projection of heaven. This is the first level. The other side is more of a conundrum: there are those who do not believe in an afterlife, there are those who are not willing to believe they are dead and there are those who die so suddenly they may need assistance from those still living. I came to know all of this that week in Virginia.

I came upon a place of transition, for those who die unsuspectingly. There are always loving helpers — call them angels or guides, etc. But it is apparently not always so easy to see them when you die. That is why we who are still living in this level can be of service. I learned this through an exceedingly illuminating and unexpected experience.

At the institute my husband, Sam, and I shared a warm and cozy room, with two single beds in opposite corners. The beds were draped with blackout curtains to block out any light during our daily meditations and for darkness in the evening.

One particular night at the institute was to revolutionize my outlook on life and death forever. It heralded a new beginning, transforming how I view death and dying. Beyond the knowledge of wisdom lies the knowing that comes from experience, and with experience came an initiation into realms which I had not previously given much thought.

I tossed and turned uneasily in my bed. My deep sleep was being disturbed by an awful coldness. I huddled up into a tight ball trying to warm myself, futilely tucking the covers right up to my face, yet the cold was unyielding, pulling me from the calm waters of my sleep. As I grudgingly became more conscious, I was bewildered with the icy coldness of the room. How had the arctic managed to reach its frosty arms into my warm haven? As I thought of getting up to put on some more clothes, fear permeated my being. An unjustifiable dread filled me as if I were on the edge of a foreboding abyss. My eyes were still closed and my body protectively snuggled up tight with my blankets.

Had I just had a nightmare? Why was I feeling fear and dread? How could I be so appallingly cold?

The intruding cold became unbearable; it brought me into a fully conscious state. Slowly I sat up on the bed, shrouded in the complete darkness of my chamber. I shivered nervously. Sam was lying in the bed adjacent to me, probably fast asleep. I thought of calling out to him, but a strange realization occurred to me. The fear was not mine; it was outside of me. Tangible, palpable, hanging in the air like cold liquid, the fear was penetrating, soaking me to my bones.

As I absorbed this information something even more chilling began. Voices cried out in the darkness, echoing and anguished.

"Help me, help me, help me," came the harrowing calls, becoming louder and louder inside my head. Or outside? Where were the cries coming from? Could Sam hear them? The cries were unyielding, disheartened, distant and close, resonating through the still night — deeply frightened calls for help.

I sat barely breathing and absolutely still in the eerie moments that followed. My heart ached for the troubled callers and pounded with uncertainty. With my eyes wide open in the darkness, an ineffable sight materialized that struck me with humility.

Hundreds of men appeared, semi-transparent, shimmering dimly in the dark. They had brought the fearful, winter chill. I was bewildered — like a dream encounter, yet this was undoubtedly real. The blackout curtain was draped before me, yet I watched them slowly moving through the room. With great clarity I noticed their dark skin and black hair. They were wearing heavy green knit sweaters and black wool pants. By their appearance I knew they were from another country. The scene was poignant and prophetic. Their dark eyes, frightened and searching, touched my eternal soul. They moved closely together, their forlorn, luminescent faces searching desperately in the unprepared ground before them. They had just died, and were now cautiously wandering the unforeseen labyrinth, finding their way home.

As this was happening I heard my husband stirring. Getting out of bed, he switched on his light. I guessed he was oblivious to what was happening as he silently left for the rest-room. His earthly movement drew their attention, the lost souls momentarily advanced toward him — or were they attracted to the dim night light he had switched on?

The men became ominously still but their ghostly calls still rang out distressingly. I sat transfixed and spellbound in the maelstrom of emotion. I silently and reverently asked for guidance and the answer calmly came.

"Tell them to go to the light." The response was instantaneously inside of me. A magnificent feeling descended into me as I realized an extraordinary light was up to my right, illuminating my peripheral vision. Awesomely powerful and beautiful I was imbued with heavenly love. Time ceased as the ubiquitous presence of Spirit filled the room.

"Go to the light," I thought. Instinctively I knew they could hear my thoughts, just as I could hear them. Slowly they moved upward, gracefully floating toward the Divine radiance. It seemed as if they were traveling a great distance, becoming smaller and smaller, before leaving my sight and disappearing into the chasm of magnificent light.

The coldness and the fear had evaporated, and now the light disappeared from my sight and I sat in quiet reverence and awe. I heard Sam come back into the room; I did not call out, but sat in tranquil equanimity, quietly absorbing the essence of what had transpired.

The light, the exquisite light, had evoked something inside me. I was close to something familiar but unreachable in my memory. A deep and consuming longing was stirring in my heart, frightening because it was so powerful and primal, and I wanted to go to the light more than anything else I had ever desired. Now it had gone, and I felt strangely abandoned. The brilliance of that love was closed off from me again, and my soul's tears slowly rolled down my cheeks, creating tiny melancholic puddles. Eventually I lay my head down upon the pillow and fell back into sleep, and was then blessed with a beautiful dream.

I woke up that morning with a deep sense of tender compassion; I knew the dream was sent to comfort and ease me through the intense emotions of the night. I will never forget it:

I know I am lying in a beautiful place. I do not see my surroundings, but I sense them. I am feeling vulnerable like a child. A man approaches me and takes me in his arms; he

*has the most beautiful, omniscient blue eyes imaginable. As
I look into them I am swept away into the depth of his
oceanic love. I know I am being held by an angel of God.
How can I contain this extraordinary love? I let it sweep
into and around me, merging with the bliss that envelopes
me and I am filled with exquisite joy. I want to hold onto it
forever, stay here forever in the euphoric love. His eyes are
pure compassion and knowing, and he smiles lovingly."*

I began to wake up, "No, I don't want to, please stay, don't
leave me." I struggled for awhile wanting to hold on, but the
dream slowly faded away. I gently released the longing with a
deep breath, as I was drawn back into this reality, and opened
my eyes.

I felt delightfully happy, fresh and new, shimmering with
the wonderful love that had embraced me. I swung the curtain
back from my bed, to see Sam rising, too.

"Let's go out for a walk," I said merrily.

Sam smiled and agreed. I hummed quietly as we dressed,
not wanting to speak yet. We silently went outside to walk in
the beautiful morning. The tall pine trees swayed about us in
the slight breeze, and the crisp air filled our lungs as we walked
hand-in-hand along the narrow country road. We were sweet
lovers sharing our night dreams. I laughed joyously as I told
him of my angel, I was filled with love. Suddenly I caught my
breath as the first image of the men came back to me. I stopped
and took Sam's arm, the images and sequence of events filling
my mind and heart with delicate sensations.

"Oh my God! Sam," I exclaimed, slightly shaking, "did
you notice anything unusual last night?" I gazed searchingly
into his eyes.

He looked at me oddly, the dramatic shift of mood

surprising. Thinking for a moment he replied, "Yes, as I got up to go to the bathroom I felt frightened — isn't that strange? The hair on my arms was standing on end, and I felt a definite unusual presence. What is it, Julie?" His caring eyes searched my strange expression.

I took a deep breath as tears filled my eyes and I related the story. The enormity of the incident triggered vast and vivid feelings. I let the heartfelt tears fall, and myriad emotions flowed through me. Sam held me lovingly as he caressed me with gentle words and kind-hearted acceptance.

The experience had been powerful and enlightening. The ethereal figures, the palpable emotion and the presence of the heavenly light all imbued an inner knowing that would never leave me. Even the dream was significant, an angel coming to hold me, soothe and comfort my aching heart and soul.

That morning was the beginning of the last day of the program I was attending. We were listening to lectures as well as intimate sharing from the other participants. As the day went on I became immersed in deep reverence. I did not feel ready to contribute what I had experienced — the impact had been so immense. Later, though, I felt compelled to tell one of the facilitators as she had noticed my somber mood. She caringly asked if she could support me in any way. Her eyes widened in surprise as I told her all the details of my night, the dark-skinned strangers from another land, new to death, wandering in shock and confusion, searching for help.

"What is it?" I asked realizing she knew something.

In town that morning she had read the sad and traumatic headlines of the newspaper.

"Julie," she said tenderly, "there was a massive earthquake in Turkey. Thousands of people were killed." She had chosen not to tell this news to the class; after all we were in a program designed to keep us unaware of the world's events for a few days. Newspapers and TV were purposely not on the property.

I now knew who those men were. The color of their skin, their clothing and the shock they appeared to be in. It made sense, but it was the innate knowing inside me that revealed the truth.

That experience was profound in many ways. I learned much and know that beyond my own reality, boundaries are not determined in the structured way I know them in the physical. The usual boundaries that limit me from hearing and seeing beyond my five senses had dissolved. I was able to detect sound inaccessible to ordinary hearing. No one else in the building had heard the lonely calls, but others had felt an eerie strangeness that night. I witnessed their souls, ordinarily inaccessible to natural sight, and I experienced their emotions. All this information had precipitated down into my reality from another dimension.

What unfolded before me was an event that happened beyond the three-dimensional world, and beyond the experience of time-space. As I watched the men move to the light it was certainly not on the same linear lines as our time-space. They traveled a great distance, getting smaller and smaller in a few moments until they were out of my view, merging with the brilliant light.

I think we must have memory circuits of feelings and words that the brain can use to interpret received thought, and so I was able to pick up and receive their thought waves. It is likely they were in a harmonious state, which allowed for the transmitting of the men's thoughts to me without a language barrier.

Many other people at the institute had peculiar sensations that night, yet no one else experienced what I did. It is still a mystery to me why I could perceive what I did; it may have depended on my clarity of mind and a higher state of frequency through meditation. I do know that the heart is a gateway to the numinous; the awesome power of love can open the heart and be a bridge to the spiritual realms. Similar experiences have happened since; it is always a breathtaking and humbling experience.

It was my persuasive hunger for self-discovery and spiritual evolvement that led me to the Monroe Institute. Here I was also to learn how to explore profound states of expanded awareness through inner journeys and visits to other energy systems and realities.

I had read Robert Monroe's first book, *Journeys Out of the Body,* after my first out-of-body experience a number of years ago, and was astonished with the extent of his journeys. I heard about the programs that were offered at the institute and became very eager to explore.

Monroe was a pioneer in the field of Human Consciousness; from 1976 he dedicated his life to exploring its potential. He first had spontaneous out-of-body experiences in 1958 when he worked as a broadcasting executive. The out-of-body experiences were just the beginning and drastically changed his life. His books are now registered as classics.

Before attending the institute you are asked to take into account that you are more than your physical body. I had been experiencing this for some time and this served as a great validation. I loved this philosophical point — it is a new notion for many, and I was ready to discover more. I had been out and away from my body yet still very much me. It is a profound realization — very liberating from the constraining attachment to the body. I also experienced many "in-body journeys," which I found to be extremely rewarding, realizing my inner world is a gateway to amazing discoveries of our universe.

I began to wonder if our fear of death would permanently disappear when we accept the impermanence of external physical existence and acknowledge we are more than our physical bodies. Without that fear can we more readily accept each moment of our life, and recognize our physical bodies as awesome vehicles that carry us through an amazing adventure on Earth? I find that this resonates as truth for me. With each new other-worldly experience my physical existence here and now is enhanced. I traverse an incredible amount of emotion and feeling as I learn, and as the collage of the universe is revealed I evolve with greater capacity to love and accept.

As I journeyed beyond our reality I began to think more and more about time and space. Is the future an illusionary concept created by the rational mind, I wondered? In many of the books that I had read, the theory of past, present and future all happening on one continuum had intrigued me. We know time exists for us in this reality, but what is beyond us and our concepts of time? Is that also accessible to us — can I experience the future now?

I incorporated in my meditations what I learned at the institute and had many fascinating journeys and discoveries. I would like to share two stories now.

I gently close my eyes to begin my meditation. I have no particular purpose but to deepen my awareness and strengthen my concentration, but it is a time when I was exploring other levels of reality and I made an intention to be open to possibilities of learning and guidance.

Soon my gross physical body is no longer part of my awareness as my consciousness expands outward. I am in alpha state, my brain waves slower, relaxed and yet aware. This is a state most of us are in when we are very relaxed and before we go to sleep. I go deeper, letting go of thoughts as they try to fill my mind with chatter. I am allowing myself to drift close to emptiness where I begin to focus my intention. I sense vast space around me and in me and I know I am part of it all. I shift my intention from this perspective and I consciously go to a familiar location, a crossing place, where I move from vastness to the ethereal, spiritual realms.

I see light all around me, and a small glowing golden bridge is visible. I am drawn toward it by its spiritual radiance and elegant simplicity. Although I want to cross, I cannot. I know I am to sit down and meditate. A tall, luminous being is beside me, helping to increase my energy frequency. I sense this is what is happening, as no other communication is taking place. On the other side of the bridge are many other celestial light beings waiting patiently for me to cross. I have been here many times before on my journeys. With unspoken trust I walk across the bridge and enter a beautiful garden of light. I leave behind my world of limitations and patiently wait for what is to be revealed.

It is different here; it is not an emotional realm. However, I am not disengaged from what I see, either. I am compassionately connected. I have surrendered to a higher knowing, trusting implicitly what unfolds, witnessing what is, without my own agenda.

Suddenly, I find myself looking down at a quiet solitary beach, the crashing waves creating a lonely melancholic hum. A middle-aged man is lying still in the golden sand, staring pensively into the immense blue sky above. He has a handsome face adorned with a full mustache and beard, but he looks regretful and anxious. I appear above him. I do not know how he perceives me, but he acknowledges me by looking at me and I sense his apprehension. Later I wonder how I must have looked to him. Did I have the image of my physical body, or was I a strange shimmering light appearing above him? I ask through thought who he is, what has happened, and I get some answers as I experience his thought waves. He looks at me with expectation. I know he is waiting for his wife and child. His boat ship-wrecked. He cannot recall where they are, or exactly what has happened. I know he is unaware he has died; he is confused and mystified as he watches me.

"Come with me," I said, or thought! He is hesitant, bewildered. He knows something is amiss, yet he is unable to figure it out. Desperate to locate his family, he is willing to reach out to me for help. Cautiously he relinquishes his place on the sand, he floats up toward my outstretched hand and we move together, instantly arriving at a park.

The park is a meeting place of sorts, a place to rest, readjust and reorganize oneself after death. As soon as we get there, he excitedly calls out, "Mother!" He is gone, disappearing into the misty light.

I stay at the park for a while. There are many people dressed in white clothes practicing Tai Chi; it looks fluid and graceful as they all move in synchronicity. There is a building with a tower and I go to it — it is a replica of the Monroe Institute. As I move to the tower I see Brian, a friend of mine and we nod to acknowledge one another. He leaves and shortly afterward I do, too.

I open my eyes and I am on my bed, my meditation and journey over. Later that day I see Brian. As we meet each other we hug.

"I saw you at the tower," he says excitedly, quite a contrast from the blasé acknowledgment in the other realm.

"Yes, I was there." I smile.

I am happy he remembers, and we talk about the differences of meeting over there versus here. We did not hug or laugh or say anything that we may in this reality. It was unemotional — it just was.

I wonder when, in our time, these events took place. Had the man on the beach been there a while, in our past, or had it just happened? I did not find any clue in his clothing. My sense was he had been there a long time. If that was so, what if I could access the future? Could I experience myself, or my family? I put this thought aside, imagining the extremely emotional and possibly disturbing feelings I may have knowing what is to come. The thought had come to my mind though; I made an intention to have the experience if there was any benefit to come from it. Then I let the thought go.

Shortly after making the intention I was moved to tears after experiencing an intimate event with my mother in meditation.

I gently close my eyes, move into an expanded state of consciousness and allow myself to float in the comfortable darkness behind my eyelids.

As I do so, I lose my physical awareness, transcend the ordinary boundaries of body and ego and am in an ethereal land. I am met at the luminous golden bridge and slowly move over to the other side, welcomed and safe. The light beings are always there; I am aware of them close by, although I do not always see them after I move away from the light garden. I move to a place I experience as soft, pink and loving. It is a place of transition for those who have just died and left their physical bodies.

I sense I am moving again and the environment changes. A deep blue sky is above me, and the surroundings have an earthly quality too them. I see a lady sitting on a wall in the distance. She is bent slightly forward; it takes but a moment to realize it is my mum. She looks younger than she is now, about thirty; she is beautiful yet looks so tired. In a moment I am there closer to her. I do not shout or run to her with open arms; I slowly move and sit beside her. I am feeling an awesome sense of peace. I know as I see her, this is how it will be when she dies, for I also know that it is not happening in our present time. I experience the intuitive knowing and non-attachment of the higher spiritual realms. There is unconditional love present, not tears or sadness or even excitement at seeing her that there would be in our normal reality. We sit together and communicate for a while, with no need to talk. Thoughts and feelings float through us. A quiet understanding resonates between us; she is waiting for something, too tired to understand what that is. I do not know what it is either, but I sit and wait with her.

I become aware of how she dies. She tells me about her father, stories she has not shared before. She unquestionably understands so much — now she is just to wait.

As we sat there I was acutely aware of her exhaustion, but I enjoyed our closeness. It was different than I know in my physical body and reality — I felt love for her, and it was so free, beyond the constraints of the mind and ego that often wants something in return. Love was a glorious energy that had nothing to do with me, or her. Nothing disturbed the beautiful ocean of love; it was pure and unconditional.

I got a sense she wanted to leave, to move on. I felt the air electrify and a radiant singing filled the space around us as the most beautiful sight lit up and illuminated the sky above us.

My great-grandmother, my mum's nana, appeared high up in the sky. Magnificently adorned with incredible angel wings spanning out gloriously behind her, she slowly descended. I could see the soft, white feathers, layered and full, gently moving as she gracefully approached us. She floated down and with her majestic wings swept up my mother into her breast, enfolding the soft celestial arms around her. With my mother safely embraced at her heart, she glided upward and out of sight. I sat mesmerized by the beautiful expression of divine love.

I came back to an ordinary state of consciousness, tears of joy and gratitude rolling down my cheeks. That was the most powerful and beautiful heavenly vision I had experienced. I did not question the reality of it, through grace I knew its truth.

About a year later I was thrilled to spend three weeks with my mum. We live in different countries and barely get to see each other once a year. A lot had happened over the years — our relationship was strained and we were not as close as I longed to be. Through both of our efforts she was able to come to America, and we spent this wonderful time together. We talked about many things, one of them death, and dying. I asked her what her beliefs were, and she really was not sure. She had a little fear about her own death and so she did not think about it. I asked her, "If someone was there for you after you die, who do you think that may be?" It was a peculiar question. She did not say anything straight away but looked at me, tilting her head downwards and raising her eyebrows. I recognized this familiar look — she was wondering why I was asking, but also she could sense that I had something on my mind, more than curiosity. It felt right that I tell the story of my meeting with her. As I told her Gran came down with huge celestial angel wings, embraced her and took her up to heavenly heights, tears came to her eyes and her whole body relaxed.

"That is beautiful; that feels so right." she said softly.

As we shared deeply we became closer. She talked a lot about the death of her parents, how painful it was and still is for her. It dawned on me just how little people talk about death and dying, and how so many people keep these feelings and fears tucked away inside. We both experienced freedom from emotions and fear as we talked about death. I could feel a release and knew this experience was healing on a deep emotional level for both of us.

Death and dying are such surreptitious subjects, yet the certainty of our life is our death! Our identity with a separate sense of self, or our ego, can keep us in a state of suffering in life, and afterward. Many other cultures view dying through very different lenses. The *Tibetan Book of the Dead,* for example, talks about the Bardo States. Bardo is an intermediate state, or a transitional state of experience. This beautiful spiritual text discusses the first state after death as ultimate consciousness. We move into the divine light. This is a given for all of us — although it seems we may need help to get there. As we enter the luminosity we experience the "Clear Light of Reality." We are absorbed back into the purity of oneness. According to this text we do not stay here, but have forty-nine days before rebirth. Our karmic propensities — our grasping, aversions and desires, eventually bring us back to another body, stricken with amnesia of the glory we have encountered. Here again we become encapsulated by ego, and another human journey until we realize our true nature, and remember who we are. This is Christ's *anamnesis.* The Hindu's call this, *smara,* the Buddhists *smriti,* the Sufi *zikir.* All translated as "remembrance." The journey of remembrance, back to oneness, is our human experience.

One does not have to believe in rebirth, of course. The beauty of freedom from fear of death is liberating in itself. We die to each moment: the beauty is to awaken to the next moment and experience it fully. As I opened myself up to possibilities, my life came alive with striking and wonderful realizations.

Chapter Two

First Lessons
of the
Other Side

*Until we accept the fact that life itself
is founded in mystery, we shall learn nothing.*
-Henry Miller

I WAS FIFTEEN WHEN THE BEAUTIFUL practice of meditation
quietly made its entrance into my life, bringing with it
silent gifts and lending a guiding hand. I look back and see
how blessed I was. This practice would become the grounding
force as I opened up to other dimensions and began to see the
hidden mysteries of life and death. It was many years before I
studied meditation's ancient roots, the wisdom and profundity
of it. My first taste came through practicing Aikido with my
father. My father is a master and teacher of this gentle and
graceful martial art. The three characters translated means, "The
way of unity with the fundamental force of the universe." It is a
discipline for perfecting the spirit. I remember the calming
meditation of our sitting before practice and how easily this
resonated with me. We opened up to the earth energies below,
the universe above and centered in our core. This was a
powerful exercise that I remembered a few years later when I
began to practice meditation on my own. I found similarities to
the prayers and my intimate conversations with God I had
when I was very young, but meditation was silent. No questions, no answers — stillness prevailed, and how I liked that!

My relationship with God as a young child was innocent and lovely. I was about six when I began praying and talking to God. I was always aware of the Omnipresence as someone I could talk to, but I knew he was not actually a being in the same sense that I experienced myself. He certainly was not the image I received at church of an old man sitting on a throne with a long white beard, surrounded by slaughtered lambs and judging us for everything we did. Although I am sure this was not the image the church wanted to convey, in my child mind this is sadly what I received. When I was eleven my family stopped going to church on Sunday morning. We were much more likely to go out into the countryside for picnics, frolic in the bubbling stream and laugh and play as we walked in the woods. I continued to feel God's presence, but organized religion was not a prevalent force or influence in my life.

I was brought up in the small village of Tynemouth in Northern England, which sits quietly on the pretty sand coast. It was a wonderful place, although I did not appreciate its unique beauty until I left seeking adventure at age seventeen, and then returned a year later. Golden sand dunes roll along the coast. There are small bays and cozy beaches. The remnants of an ancient castle still grandly stand over the small village with rugged cliffs dropping down toward the immense blue-gray sea. The main street is lined with small shops, bakeries and boutiques, and lots of pubs with picturesque flowerboxes adorning the walls. I loved to watch the raging wild seas, huge waves crashing rigorously into the enduring shore on grave stormy days. If the skies shone with warm and brighter sunshine, instead of the almost ubiquitous grey clouds, I may have stayed. Tynemouth is timeless in a way, not much seems to change, and this too adds to its beauty and charm. Many young people leave, only to return in later years to set up their family home. When I return now, I love to reminisce while walking around the old village and along the seafront. Found childhood memories surface, as well as the early visions and strange experiences I had.

The scenic drive to the countryside took no more than thirty minutes, and come rain or shine, usually rain, we would go for walks and excursions enjoying the outdoors or the comfort of a village inn. I loved to sip Coke through a tall straw while watching the drizzle splashing patterns on the windows, hoping for the rain to stop so we could explore outside. My appreciation and love of nature was greatly inspired by these times.

When I left home at seventeen, I traveled to California, the very named conjuring up images of sunshine and freedom. Like a butterfly emerging from its cocoon, I was drawn to spread my wings and discover the world for myself. The beautiful beaches, nearby mountains and deserts called to me. The year was full of adventure, exploring new places and trying new things, a wild and carefree time of laughter and excitement.

At eighteen when I returned home I began to practice my meditation again just for a short while before going to sleep. Coming back to England was not easy — my parents had immigrated to the Canary Islands. My life was drastically different from what I imagined I would return to. Apart from what I carried in my suitcase, everything I ever owned had gone, taken from our home when my parents moved. But it was my home itself, the epicenter of connection and love, with all the memories, the security I had taken for granted, all disbanded, which exposed my heart to loneliness. I remember the cold winter; the wind howling outside, yet a peaceful yearning flickered in my heart. Something deep within stirred an echo of remembrance, which encouraged me to listen. Sitting in my small flat I began to meditate at night. The stillness and peace was a welcomed friend and I learned to let go of the longing for my home of the past.

It was during this time I started to sense an unusual aware-ness at the crown of my head. I am not sure if this just presented itself one night or if it was a gradual realization. This peculiar feeling was quite an enigma. It felt like I had openings that led into the "unknown." It was as if, when taking my awareness into my head, I could see doorways, that if I focused on one, I would be whisked away into another realm and be initiated into great secrets of the universe. It was strange for me at that time to think that within me was a vastness, an entryway into space, or an access to ghostly and extraordinary realms. There was an edge here for me, for I was inquisitive, yet I was very much alone on my spiritual journey. My family had left the country so I did not have my father to consult, and at the time it did not seem relevant to mention that I meditated even to friends. It was my private practice, a sacred inner journey, and so it would only be my partner at that time, Steve, who would know. The edge was that of isolation and misunderstanding from others, versus finding my own identity and being true to myself.

I always had a deep yearning for more of life, and a knowing that the yen was of a spiritual nature. I began my journey alone, meditating, moving into silence, quietness and stillness, and just observing what, if anything, arose and was revealed to me. I would not want to share this sacred practice in fear of been misunderstood by my friends. Meditation was not something I heard anyone talk about. When I became conscious of these doorways, perceiving the imperceptible, I was cautious and surprised. I did not expect anything, you see; I was just observing, like witnessing the innocence of butterflies around the peach orchid. Sensing a presence behind these openings only caused me to be more cautious. I felt that I could enter just by focusing on the doorways, or I could let in the presence behind them. What would it be like to be the butterfly? And what if the trees were not laden with fruit?

At that time I chose to be cautious. I had met Steve on my return to England, and we had a close, loving relationship for the next ten years. Steve would sense my slightly altered state of consciousness as I sat meditating, and the energy that descended was almost palpable — it would stir quite an anxious feeling in him as he watched me. So I would respect his feelings and did not delve into the mysteries that unfolded before me. Also, his trepidation spooked me a little. We had no idea what may have been waiting on the other side. Later I learned of the spiritual opening in the crown (the top of the head), the magnificent realizations of the Absolute (or what is known as God, or cosmic consciousness), and the ultimate reality of unity. But it seemed I had work to do first.

The spiritual unknown and mystical experiences are understandably frightening to many. We can encounter dark archetypal forces, confront our own fear of death and there is always the lurking question of our sanity; yet there is much splendid mystery and insight to behold. Organized religion, for the most part, has sadly lost its mystical roots, becoming institutionalized. It blinds us from the whole truth with its dogma, doctrines and strict disciplinary measures. Ghosts are usually portrayed as frightening and evil, or we are told they cannot exist. Death is rarely discussed, except in fear-based religion where the threat of damnation is ever-present! The mystical realms are left for wise sages or mystics of indigenous cultures. Why? Not so long ago in the Middle Ages those who had spontaneous mystical experiences were condemned as witches or sorcerers — tortured and put to death. Today these experiences are stigmatized with labels of pathologies or ridiculed as delusions by those who do not experience them, whose beliefs may be challenged or who are unwilling to be open to possibilities.

I believe we are each a drop of the vast ocean of the universe, yet never separate from the ocean itself, each of us having the drama of the cosmos in our very selves. The spiritual realms lie within us: strange indescribable dimensions, rich cosmic mysteries and other worldly beings. I found so much of these waiting to be explored and revealed as my boundaries dissolved and I moved into the exploration of my consciousness, the mystery of my being.

The healing potential of inner exploration is huge; within us all is the possibility of profound healing and peace. We are part of the magnificence of creation, but we may need to revise our spiritual beliefs a little, or dramatically, for us to tap into the intelligence of the universe. There are powers and energies of this planet that are beyond most of our comprehension at this time. Discarnate beings, entities, archetypes and deities exist in radically different realms. Ecstatic joy can be found, but also frightening experiences are possible without a framework or support system to rely on. I would always recommend a teacher for beginning a spiritual practice — someone to talk to and have as a guide. Yet as one moves deeper the true teacher, the vastness of the true nature of the mind, is the guide, for within us all lies the truth.

There are many paths to travel that are full of rich and insightful teachings. Greek Mythology, the history of Western thought from Plato and Aristole, Buddhism, Hinduism, Chrisitian Mysticism and Sufism to name just a few, offer the teachings of wisdom and compassion with many years of tradition. One does not have to get caught in the religious dogma or doctrines to reach the underlying truth and richness of such teachings.

At eighteen I was uneducated about other dimensions and the inner vast awareness that is who I am. Energy, transcendence of this reality and so forth were a foreign language to me. My hesitation not to go further at that time was not just due to my naïveté and apprehension but my inner wisdom, guiding me to explore at a later point in time. Enjoying my meditation in stillness and quietude was like sailing on a bountiful, lily-laden lake. Later I would come to witness many kinds of extraordinary phenomena. My meditation practice may have opened me up to some of the mysteries and bizarre experiences of this world, or maybe I was born with a peculiar gift and such experiences would have presented themselves no matter what. But the sitting grounded me and gave me a steady base to witness the unusual. Anyway, I began to grow, to learn, to expand and increase my awareness before reaching a wonderful fruition, where I transcended the edge and began to share my stories. My biggest hurdle was to get over the fear of annihilation. I could not understand this irrational fear of death if I revealed my truth and shared my experiences. Later in the book I will share the intuitive story that led to a dramatic demise of the fear.

Sitting quietly, watching TV one evening with friends, I calmly stood up.

"My nana has died," I said softly. "I need to go home."

I have always been very perceptive and sensitive. I trusted my intuition, sometimes I just knew things, like most of us experience sometimes, but it was difficult to explain how. My heart was often clear as a mirror.

When I returned to my apartment I found a message to call my brother. I already knew what it was about. The emotion then hit me, of course, and I cried through the night. I was nineteen and had recently returned to America. At that time it was also difficult for me to fly home to England. I was not sure what I would do. I wanted to return for the funeral, yet if I did it would be unlikely that I would return to the States. I was waiting for a visa renewal, and the thought of returning to England scared me. I was in the midst of a very difficult period in life. I was not sure where I was going. I felt lost, without direction, but what I intuitively knew was America was in my heart and would be my home. The following day my decision to stay and not fly back to England for the funeral came about unexpectedly.

I was lying curled up like a ball on the sofa, gently crying, my heart was aching with the sad loss of Nana. Sweet memories of us dancing together through life were flowing away like water, her touch never to be tasted again. I thought I would have to go back to England to find closure at her funeral. I wanted to say goodbye and be with my family to ease the pain. An unusual mood descended down into the room as I continued to cry. It had an ethereal, unearthly feel, and a wonderful sense of equanimity filled me. I knew without a doubt my nana was there, smelling her distinct body scent. I could not see her nor hear her, but I could feel her unmistakable presence. Overcome with love, I did not think to question it, and my heart opened as I accepted her being there. I began feverishly to talk to her, releasing my feelings of love and guilt, but she stopped me. I did not need to explain — she knew, she understood, and she loved me unconditionally. I experienced immeasurable gifts. My mind was filled with blooming chrysanthemums like those that abundantly lavished her garden. I smiled, my tears continued, but without so much grief this time. Miraculously I was embraced by her enduring spirit and calmed by her heavenly presence. I knew I had been given a beautiful chance to say goodbye to my nana, whom I dearly loved. I am so grateful I was open to perceive her energy. It is possible for all of us to be open to energy of lost ones as they pass away. It may just be a matter of being open to it perceptually, thinking of them, and feeling into our own heart. If they are able, they will be there. Talk to them and joyously open your heart. Everyone's experience will be different, but there are numerous possibilities. A great gift and delightful experience of joy is to know that death is not the end but a point of transition for the soul.

When my other nana died quite a few years later, I had a beautiful encounter with her, too. Before she actually died, though, I had an interesting insight. On going to bed one evening I heard the telephone ring, and the thought at the back of my mind was, "That's my dad calling, Nana's died." I heard only one ring, and I did not pull the thought up too consciously, for I was mistaken about the phone ringing and it was an intuition I would rather deny. The following morning the phone did ring, it was my dad with news of my nana's death.

I spent time crying, feeling the loss and talking to her hoping she could somehow hear me. Suddenly I felt a beautiful energy filling the space around me. I experienced it like blissful pink mist dancing merrily and cascading around me. There was joy and freedom — it was tangible and so beautiful it caused me to laugh out loud in surprise. I could intensely sense Nana's presence; I knew she had come to me to express her exquisite joy as she transcended from this world. She stayed with me for a while. It was beautiful to have her at my home, as she had never been there and it felt great to be able to share it with her. I felt her happiness for me. The experience touched me deeply, and when I flew home for her funeral, the essence of her joy and the celebration I felt at home in America never left me. I saw her petite body in the funeral home, lying so still and graceful. I understood our physical body as a transient vehicle in which our soul travels in this world, and received a deeper sense of knowing that we are so much more than this, that the journey of our life here is temporary and is to live as fully as we can.

I have always been blessed with wonderful friends who have never questioned my experiences, but have been open to the possibilities and have often been inspired to begin their own spiritual journeys.

I met my husband Sam in 1994. He was a successful businessman and deeply entrenched in that world. Our lives appeared to be poles apart, yet something drew us together and our friendship began. Each week we met for lunch and shared what was happening in our lives at that time. Sam turned around companies, and I loved to hear the insights and workings of the business world. Drawn to my connection of Spirit, he loved to hear my stories of adventure in consciousness and in the spiritual realms. Our friendship blossomed, and we spent four amazing years traveling together around the world while exploring mountains, jungles, deserts and other cultures. Our deepest connection, though, came through our exploration of consciousness together; Sam decided to leave the business world behind for a while, searching for deeper meaning and a spiritual framework that would change his life drastically. He witnessed many of my spiritual encounters, intrigued and fascinated by what unfolded. There was little space for doubt; when an authentic expression of the mysterious universe unfurls, a deep resonance occurs, a gentle reminder of all of our potential.

Chapter Three

Pink Beings
and *Entities*

*Our normal waking consciousness, rational consciousness as
we call it, is but one special type of consciousness, whilst all
about it, parted from it by the filmiest of screens there lie the
potential forms of consciousness entirely different.*
–William James

THE UNIVERSE CONTINUED TO SHOWER ME with extraordinary insights. I explored mysterious realms, saw many unusual things and experienced phenomenon that are beyond my imagination. I have laughed and cried, become confused and gained clarity. At times I was so overwhelmed with the extent of what occurred I would throw my arms up to the sky and say, "God, what is all this about?" And I would be answered with something as unexplainable as ever, and so I quickly learned to take it all in my stride, knowing with time I would understand.

I love the desert in its many forms, be it golden sand dunes that roll softly toward the distant horizon, or the rugged rocks that host homes to lizards, snakes and other curious creatures. There are so many desert landscapes to be explored, ablaze with the richness and diversity of nature. Evening, with her unmistakable sunsets, is always a time of beauty and serenity. The harshness of the desert is softened as the fluid colors paint and spill splendidly through sky. Throughout time the desert has been a place of mystery, magic and revelations. I find it a place for quiet and solitude away from the often noisy and busy world I live in. To be away from the city lights is to be graced with the evening's heavenly skies. Full of stars, planets and expansiveness, it is a time to feel the humility of my place in the infinite universe.

I once spent a week walking in silence in Death Valley, California. The unique and unsympathetic landscapes tested my body, mind and spirit with unyielding, brutal frankness and intense, unforgiving heat. Yet the seduction of the desert with her passionate honesty elicited self-reflection, and enabled me to find my own dusty truths and resolutions. Eventually, after enduring the hot, dry days with thoughts screaming aloud in my head, the continuing chatter of my mind quieted down so that I could hear behind thoughts and quietly listen to my heart speak. It was humbling as my abhorring ego settled down and accepted the seemingly hostile environment, and I could be at total peace with who I was and where I was.

Journeys to the desert do not have to be so intense, of course. Enjoying a weekend of relaxation at the hot springs in Palm Desert, California is also enticing. This was why Sam and I were here one particular weekend. After spending a few hours soaking in the hot tubs, we watched the glowing serenity of sunset as luscious reds and oranges filled the desert sky. When darkness descended, we walked out into the night, away from the lights of the hotel, to enjoy the solitude, stillness and melodious sounds of the night. We chose a couple of sturdy rocks that would grant us comfort to sit and watch the clear indigo sky. The shimmering stars floating in the immeasurable universe above drew our eyes upward. Underneath the sounds of the creatures of the night, I could hear the quiet stillness, vast and inviting. I tuned into my body and breath, presencing myself to encounter the beauty and exquisiteness of each moment. I was conscious of my beating heart, graciously pumping life force through me, feeding and nourishing every cell. I journeyed inward, feeling and sensing my body, and then outward, my consciousness expanding, connecting to the night and stillness and feeling part of it.

I sat enjoying the evening for some time, and I do not know what prompted me, but I glanced down and was captivated with an amazing, breathtaking sight.

A pink being, an entity so beautiful so incredibly lovely, was moving outward from my chest. I was awe-struck and enchanted with the remarkable and amazing spectacle. It moved about eight inches from my heart, leaning outward from me but still connected. Its skin was smooth, translucent, ethereal and the softest, loveliest pink I had seen. Its shape was like a small baby but without the familiar features — just two lines delineated gently closed eyes. I continued to stare in astonishment, still awestruck, until it gracefully floated back into my body. I looked up to the sky, intoxicated with mystery, to ask, "God, what was that?"

I did not have time to ask because I was met with another astonishing sight that filled me with exhilaration. A beautiful complex of harmoniously interweaving lines of energy, like soft laser beams of light, were radiating through the night sky. The thought came to me that these were prayers, meditations and wishes moving to their intended destinations before precipitating down into physical reality. Never had I seen anything like it, so beautiful and mesmerizing that my breath was momentarily taken from me.

"Sam, do you see that?" I whispered.

"What?" he replied, looking at me.

"The streams of light . . . look, look, golden rivers flowing through the sky."

Sam was looking up at the sky, but he could not see the lights. I continued to quietly describe the amazing sight with tears gently rolling down my cheeks. Soon all the lights began to fade and I was left to watch the inky blackness of space with its generous sprinkling of sparkling stars. My heart ached with joy and longing. I wanted desperately for Sam to share the wonder that I had just seen, the exotic mysteries igniting my questioning mind.

"That isn't all, Sam." I began to laugh. I told him of the beautiful pink creature in my heart. His eyes widened in surprise and wonder.

"What do you think it is, Sam? Is this my soul, my spirit? Does it silently sleep in my heart as I journey through life, patiently waiting for me to awaken? Is this how our soul looks?"

Neither of us had an answer to my questions, but I continued to wonder if this is the part of me that I am aware of traveling out of my body at night. Does it silently leave to nourish itself in the knowing of the universe and fall back to sleep as it returns to my body, leaving me ignorant of the adventure? I wondered if this is the essence of who I am, beyond the physical body. And the lights I saw . . . Wow, what an extraordinary sight!

We discussed energy and matter, two different manifestations of a universal substance. Our thoughts are energy, vibrating at a much higher frequency than physical matter. Was I seeing bands of communication vibrating beyond the distinctive physical expression we know? Do our prayers move through the sky at incredible speed and somehow became visible to my naked eye, or was I glimpsing another dimension that is interwoven in ours, where our thoughts are expressed? So many inexplicable questions and puzzlements remained. I was captivated, though, with the delight and profound enigma of the mystery.

It was a few months later that I experienced a pink being again. Its unexpected, eloquent arrival nourished me with its cosmic presence.

This particular evening I was driving home from Los Angeles, down through the canyon to my Laguna Beach home. It had been an emotionally charged evening for me. I was studying for a degree in human behavior. The content of the course was at times very intense and brought forward old wounds, bringing opportunities to heal. I needed desperately to cry — the emotion was welling up inside me until I could not hold back my tears any longer.

Maybe I should have pulled over to the side of the road as the crying began to break through. However, I continued to drive. I felt bleak and alone in the pain I was feeling but then appeared the sweetest sight I could have possibly hoped for.

I saw a familiar pink light descending from the dimly lit sky to my left. A beautiful celestial being flew gracefully down from the heavens, through the side of the car and into the passenger seat beside me. I was utterly surprised and more surprised still at my response. I continued to cry, as if the miracle of what I was seeing escaped me, but it did not. This extraordinary vision warmed my heart. The enchanting being was so beautiful to behold, and I was immersed in waves of gratitude and love. As I witnessed this, I realized it was a sacred gift, a sight of what is usually hidden from us, and I continued to be in the moment of my humanness, feeling pain, yet grateful and humble. I knew it was not meant to shock me out of my process of healing, but to be a guide, to keep me safe. I was energetically and lovingly held by this magical entity. I was protected as I continued to cry. Sobs of sadness mixed with bursts of laughter because the rapturous and precious angel accentuated the strange and wonderful journey home. I felt absolutely present to each moment, fully conscious to my experience of pain and marvel, present and awake to my experience, with a deep sense of compassion.

When I arrived home, I collapsed in tears and Sam held me. I do not think he had ever seen me so upset, with so many emotions flowing through me. I was experiencing hurt from old wounds and memories, and wonder from the inexplicable mysteries that life holds. A deep longing stirred within me to reconnect to something that would make sense of all the uncertainty of the world, and I sensed it was so close and yet out of reach.

Later when I had calmed myself, a wonderful peace descended over me. I realized what I already really knew — I am never alone. Even when the illusion of aloneness overcomes me, I unequivocally know I am never alone. It is so liberating to see what is usually hidden beyond the five senses. It seems to be at times of the heart, when I am feeling love or vulnerable and open that I see strange things, shattering my concepts of the limited world we live in.

About two years after seeing the first pink being, I met a lady who had some answers for me. She is a physicist and also a clairvoyant. A fascinating woman, she grew up in Japan with her grandfather, a master of Feng Shui. As a child she was able to see energy and her grandfather encouraged her to explore her intuition and insight. As he taught her about Feng Shui, she understood at a very deep level, as she could see exactly what he was talking about. Over many years she studied the energy she was experiencing in many forms. She eventually came to the West for her undergraduate and graduate degrees in physics. Marie sensed it would be unlikely her clairvoyance would be accepted in the scientific field, and so she became very well known for her "hunches." She continued to study Feng Shui, and that is how I came to meet her. My husband and I asked her to come and Feng Shui our home; we were interested in maximizing the energy to enhance our family life. As I realized she was clairvoyant I asked if she had ever seen anything that looked like a pink being in the heart area.

"Oh, yes," she said. I was thrilled.

"Please tell me about that," I said excitedly.

"As the heart chakra is activated the petals open. Many people think this is an open heart. But there are smaller petals inside that rarely open. If they do, they blossom a beautiful pink. It could be seen as a tiny pink being."

I briefly told her about the pink being I saw and she beamed. "That's wonderful; the inner petals of your heart are very open. Isn't it wonderful to see your soul!"

I was overjoyed to have validation for what I had seen. We talked more and when I gave her permission, she began to take a look at my other chakras.

We all have seven major energy centers located up and down the spine, in and above the brain, and located in the subtle bodies that entwine the physical body. The word chakra literally means "wheel."

Each chakra is a distinct center of energy and experience with its own sound syllable, color, element and frequency. The physical externalizations of each are connected to a body system or organ. Each chakra has emotional, mental, psychic and spiritual attributes.

Marie told me my sixth chakra, or third eye was open —
this is what I have been calling my inner vision. Even though I
had read and studied much material on the chakras, clairvoyance and psychic phenomena, I had never met anyone who
knew and understood the varied experiences that I have had. I
began to feel very excited as I realized I had found a teacher to
help me on my journey, or at the very least a person with whom
I could share stories and who could empathize with what I
experienced.

It was a few months later I saw my own energy centers,
possibly as they exist, or possibly the symbol of how my brain
interprets them. Either way it was an intriguing and insightful
look into the hidden sources of the mysterious influences of my
life. The sixth energy vortex at the center of my brow was vivid
and entrancing. As I looked in the mirror at my face, I began to
see a revealing, multi-dimensional image. Two spinning
vortices appeared enticing me with their anonymity. Indistinct
in color but reminiscent of thick misty gray whirlpools,
touching at the thinnest points and spinning outward in opposite directions, they flooded my vision. It was
multi-dimensional, for they were not exactly in or on my forehead, but existing on a plane of existence beyond time and space,
co-existing with this plane of reality, interweaving through and
beyond my physical body, appearing to be huge and yet covering
a measurably small area of my forehead.

Often chakras are symbolized as lotus flowers, with various
numbers of colorful petals. It is difficult to articulate and describe
their actual visual presence. The lotuses represent images that
were created so people could relate. The images of lotus flowers,
with their distinct amount of petals for each chakra, are beautiful
and sacred maps to direct us into these dimensions of energy
within us.

Sedona is another desert location that I am drawn to that has been a place of mystery and delight. Nestled in the heart of central Arizona 4500 feet above sea level, Sedona is a land of enchantment. As you draw near to Sedona it is the deep red color of the rocks and their unusual formations that are the most outstanding. The striking rock formations, crystalline streams and beautiful, forever-changing landscape are just the surface of what Sedona offers. But it is the wonderful energetic feeling Sedona awakens which is the most unique. It is a place where the natural electromagnetic field of the Earth is strong. The Spirit of the land calls out and it is difficult to not perceive the magical connection with the Earth here. On my first visit I was excited about hiking on the rich, invigorating trails and absorbing the natural beauty. I chose Bear Mountain to be the place of my first adventure. From my hotel room I could see the dramatic rise of the mountain up toward the bright blue sky. The terrain looked intriguing with myriad paths to explore and enjoy. As I looked at the rocks I could see images of eagles and Indians, as if nature had molded into herself the sacredness of what had lived here not so long ago.

I began in the clear early morning with my three friends. We each had a small pack with water and snacks, and excitedly we drove to the trailhead and eagerly set off on our journey. I was bursting with energy and walked speedily ahead of the others, occasionally breaking into a run and then stopping to take in the magnificent views. I was amazingly happy and felt like I was in my element, laughing spontaneously at the freedom I was feeling. I approached a good lookout point and began to walk toward the cliff edge. Being conscious of myself and surroundings, I noticed a definite change in the quality and mood of the environment. I had walked into a thick mist of sadness. I knew the feeling was outside of me, yet it was visceral and quite overwhelming as I wandered around. My stomach knotted and my heart ached as I sensed the grief. I was alone as my companions had stopped for a rest a short distance behind me. I sat down on the red earth, close to a cliff edge with a magnificent view of the desert plains and distant mountains. I sat cross-legged, musing over the present situation. I wanted to reach out to this sad energy that was all about and affecting me so. All I could think to do was to offer love. I began to meditate, centering myself in my heart until the softness of love emanated through me. I was so deeply moved by the polarity of emotions, love and sadness, that tears fell from my eyes to the ground below.

With my eyes half closed I could still see the beautiful landscape in front of me. The sadness and love flowed around and through me and the golden sun shined kindly down on my body. My attention was caught by the sound of rocks falling.

"Someone is climbing up the rock face," I thought, "but they're moving so quickly, that's not possible."

The noise got louder and closer. Suddenly the darkness of my inner vision lit up and I could miraculously and clearly see the face of the cliff below, as if I was looking directly at it and what it was that was climbing up. I gasped for air as I saw a large, dark energy mass. It was bounding up the cliff toward me, zigzagging side to side. It was round and dense resembling an intense black fireball. I was mesmerized and still as I took all of this in. Then I heard a loud, clear and uncompromising deep voice shout, "Go."

I did not stop to question it. I got up and ran! After a hundred feet or so I stopped, feeling a combination of excitement and exhilaration at what I had just seen and heard. My heartbeat was pounding in my chest. Looking back, there was nothing to be seen, but the images remained strong and lucid. I stood in the warm sun with the cool breeze softly caressing me, wondering who or what the energy mass was. I did not sense malevolence, but I got a sense that my energy had unexpectedly intruded on its privacy.

My partner had come looking for me, and had spotted me running along the cliff. He held his breath as I ran so quickly and close to the edge.

"Are you crazy?" he said when he got to me, a little shaken by my daring run.

"Maybe," I said laughing. "You'll never guess what just happened."

As we walked back down the mountain I related the story, and all the while I had the strongest sensation of being watched. I occasionally turned around but saw nothing, yet an image of a young Indian came to mind, mischievously laughing at me as I went on my way. As I sat and contemplated the experience later, it came to me that I had disturbed something. I reflected on the initial sadness that I had felt and wondered if the entity had been unable to move on from its intermediate state between death and rebirth, or from moving to a higher level? The land around Sedona was occupied by many Indians and who knows all the tragedies that occurred to them on their sacred land, and how many still remain trying to protect the land. Each time I visit this location I always say a healing prayer and hope that the sadness that had saturated the place has dispersed back into the light of love.

I was feeling so light-hearted and free in Sedona, my body invigorated from the excellent hiking, my spirit refreshed from the sheer joy of my experiences. It felt so great at the end of the day to relax in the outside Jacuzzi with friends, my body, mind and spirit integrating the events of the day.

It was that evening after my enchanting and mystical day on the rocks of Sedona that I began to see the captivating glow of auras around people again. There were five of us, good friends, sitting together enjoying each other's company. It was a lovely evening; the stars were bright and clear above our heads. The sky was inky black, the slight moon not yet showing itself from behind the surrounding mountains. Tain, our friend who lived in Sedona, was sitting on the edge of the pool telling a story, and we sat quietly listening to his soft voice. At some point I became aware of a beautiful glow about his body. I looked about for the source of this light, but could not find it. The shimmering glow continued to pull at my attention. There was something unusual about it. The color soft, translucent and green — it emanated mysteriously around his head and upper body. It appeared to be pulsating like a wave. I looked at my friend sitting next to him expecting to see the same color, but beautiful hues of purple and blue glowed and sparkled like an enchanting dance of mist around him. My eyes turned to another friend, different shades of green shimmered elegantly about him. I lifted my own arm, hoping to see something there too, and to my delight a deep blue glowed luminously around me. How stunning these mystical colors were, shining gracefully, inviting me into the mystery of being. I felt the evening was charmed, some mysterious secret being revealed to me. I did not mention it to anyone until I went to bed that evening and told my newfound secret to Steve. We sat up a few hours playing, me watching him, seeing how long I could see his colors as they pulsed around his body, and I would hold my own hand up and be captivated as the wonderful colors continued to move around me.

The following day I could still see the energy fields; they came and went from my vision, delighting and fascinating me. They would change in size and density, curiously coming and going from my vision. I was so happy to be seeing these lovely auras around people again.

When I was a child everyone had sparkling colors and lights, and the trees shone with a pink glow that made them magical and more alive. I felt like I had claimed something back that had been taken from me long ago, my gift renewed in this beautiful town called Sedona. I am not certain of my age when I stopped seeing auras, but as far as I can recall I was six or seven, and I think before that I always saw them.

Before hiking the following day I went to a metaphysical bookstore and bought what I could on energy fields as well as some other books that were significant to other strange phenomena that occurred that I will tell in later chapters. These experiences were very real to me; I began to look at my whole spiritual framework wondering where such mystery fit in. I began to change my perspective as my continued experiences broke down the illusion of the objective world and its limitations. I found other cultures and traditions that talk freely of the things that I experienced at a much deeper level. I gained knowledge that has been passed down over thousands of years and particular paths to cultivate learning. I continued to learn and explore, developing awareness, consciousness and insight.

Little did I know at that time that the books I bought that day, one by Barbara Brennan and the other by Robert Monroe, would be so influential in my life. A few years later I went to Barbara Brennan's School of Healing and learned to work with the human energy field, or aura, for the purpose of healing and learning. I also participated in the Monroe Institute's programs, exploring the possibility of other realms and dimensions, out-of-body travel, and the guiding of souls to higher realms.

Ever since that trip to Sedona I have been able to see auras again, not just around people but around all living objects. Trees are always bathed in a glimmering light, looking larger than their physical boundaries; there is an added quality and vibrancy of life. The soft pink glow around them gives them another dimension of beauty and elegance, especially when they are dancing freely in the wind. Seeing auras again ignites my childlike innocence and how wonderful and natural it was then to see colors and energy, springing forth from all of life in a sweet celebration.

I am often moved by the beauty and mystery of my sight. Watching a teacher of mine, John F. Barnes, give a speech one day, I was mesmerized by the stunning light that followed him around the podium. A purple beam of light came from above striking him in the front and back of his chest, right at heart level. It was a powerful image, reinforcing my feeling that he was talking poetically from his heart with divine guidance. I was studying his unique, powerful and effective approach to healing. Intrigued with the teachings, I continued taking classes. During one of the unwinding classes, I had the opportunity to be worked on by John and his son, with this method, the body's own intelligence, mixed with the essence of the facilitator's energy, releases its bounds, as it seeks freedom. I sat on the edge of the table as they simultaneously placed their hands on my body. Immediately, light flooded through me, and I saw with clarity, two purple beams of light and two blue, careen internally through my body. An awesome, alchemical experience of light, in which, by some inexorable law, my body moved without my mind and released its hidden anguish.

I continued to see energy in different forms, beautifully enchanting, and often quite surprising. The next encounter with an entity happened on an airplane. It was unexpected, and the most outlandish looking creature I have ever seen. If there are a lot of these energetic entities about then we should all be happy that we do not ordinarily see them.

This happened a few years later and by this time I was quite used to my inner vision opening at unexpected moments, and beholding unusual sights.

Sam and I were returning from a trip to Virginia. We had been meditating quite intensively, so I was particularly open and sensitive to energies around me. We boarded our flight to Los Angeles and settled into our seats. Shortly after take off I was sitting quietly with my eyes closed, when my inner vision registered a movement under the airplane seats. My eyelids flew open and to my alarm, a green, slimy, octopus-like creature went scurrying under the seats.

"Oh, my God!" I cried, catching my breath with an exclamation and lifting my legs aghast with horror. "What was that?" I thought.

The lady in the adjacent seat looked at me disapprovingly. "Oh lady," I thought, "If only you could see what I see."

A baby toward the front of the plane began to scream anxiously, its sensitive spirit probably sensing the unnerving creature. Children are much more open than adults; still very close and connected to the world of Spirit, their energy fields are perceptive and vulnerable. I grabbed Sam's arm.

"Did you see that?" It was a silly question — I knew he had not; he was absorbed in reading a book.

"What?" he responded curiously.

I quietly told Sam what I saw. With a surprised and appalling look on his face, he asked half-heartedly, "Can you still see it?" It really is not anything he wanted to see himself, or even know of its presence. I could see it with my inner vision now, moving under the seats toward the front of the plane.

It is truly fascinating to see these things. It really showed me how energy can manifest into form and that our thought forms actually exist and, given enough energy, precipitate down into our reality. My intuitive instinct, given the nature of it, was that it manifested through human fear and became an energy form that "feeds" off our fear. Airplanes are certainly places where that feeling exists consistently. It could have come from one person who unconsciously eliminated it, or it may have been a conglomeration of many people's thoughts over a period of time. Anyway it was a rather ugly looking thing.

As I witnessed this creature, I began to visualize similar creatures, but these were golden white, made with thoughts of love and divinity. As I created beautiful, loving, golden white forms in my imagination I perceived them embracing the dark green slimy ones with love, until they all disappeared out of my vision.

"Has it gone yet?" Sam asked curiously.

"Yes, I think so."

"Good," he replied smiling, at me, and then we both giggled at the strangeness of what we had come across.

I rarely have the sense of malevolence during an encounter, but there was a time an atrocious creature came at me during the night that gave me quite a shock.

I was fast asleep at home, immersed in my dream.

I was in England, somewhere in the countryside, sitting on a fence at the edge of a green field. I was chatting away to my friend Tony when a couple came by and asked me the way to Bethlehem. Bethlehem! I had no clue and was quite embarrassed. I had no idea where Bethlehem was; in fact, I did not even know it was in England!

A horrifyingly loud shriek startled me and pulled me from my dream. I instantly opened my eyes. The room was dark and quiet. I was lying on my stomach. "Why did I wake up so suddenly?" I remember thinking.

A sense of apprehension swept through me as I recalled the bloody scream that had pulled me from sleep, and then another spine chilling cry echoed menacingly around me. I was about to jump up but my inner vision opened, and caused me to freeze in alarm.

I could see clearly behind me the bedroom door which was ajar, the small hallway, and the kitchen entryway, just as if I were looking directly at them through the semi-darkness. Astonished, shocked and very alarmed from the horrid shriek, I lay still and another startling sight appeared. An amazing, spinning, black and gray tunnel formed, smoky and sinister. It was about two feet in diameter, and it came from high up through the ceiling in the hall and down through my bedroom doorway into the room, stopping a few feet above me. Another terrifying scream shattered the quiet night. Like the call of a shrieking banshee it heralded the arrival of some ominous creature. I remained motionless as I watched this unfold. I realized this tunnel, a dark and eerie opening from another realm, was a means for whatever was coming to precipitate down into my world without care or concern for my well being. Then the rather distressing vision of a crazy spiraling black crow came hurtling down the tunnel toward me. It had no clear features, but the edges of this gruesome thing were ragged, madly quivering and spinning so fast that it looked like crow feathers in a ferocious frenzy. Still frozen by this outlandish sight I lay still and the creature came right at me, landing on my back, its nasty claws grabbing my shoulders, burning my skin.

"Do you believe in Black Magic?" it screamed hideously in my ear. So eerie and sinister, its high-pitched scream I will never forget. My body was begging me to flee but a wiser, knowing part of me, crazily unaffected, said silently, "Do not be frightened."

I lay precariously still in the wavering moments that followed. As I observed this mad hideous creature gripping onto my back, its heat penetrating my skin, I was aware of the duality of my being — calm presence and fright. The creature's repugnant breath was wafting close to my ear, coveting some reaction. I could sense that it wanted me to be afraid, as if this was not obvious with its screaming arrival and menacing call in my ear of Black Magic! I remained motionless, but I could feel my heart pounding heavily in my chest. I had found my center and was able to remain calm. I believed it could not hurt me and was not certain it wanted to, but it did want some reaction from me. The heat continued to penetrate my back, still burning, until its claws loosened their hostile grip and the thing went ricocheting backward up through the tunnel. The spinning tunnel disappeared into itself, and as quickly as it began, it was over.

A little shaky, I apprehensively sat up. My back was still hot and prickling. It was then, sitting alone in the darkness of my room, I let a little fear slowly sink into me. A strange unworldly creature flying into my room through a doorway from another dimension . . . I was not ready to fall back to sleep, nor did I desire another encounter. With my eyes wide and searching, I got up to find my boyfriend, Steve, who had fallen asleep in another room. I woke him, needing some human contact, and explained what had happened. He looked at me horrified.

"Oh, my God! That's incredible. Are you okay?" He looked at my back. It was red and hot but otherwise unscathed.

We had no idea what it could have been; we guessed an indiscriminate hit-and-miss from a deranged creature, seeing if it could unhinge me from my sanity. It got lucky with its chosen prey, for I saw and felt it, but if it was fear it was after, it would have to go else where. We continued to talk about it for a little while, as it was so unusual, and the more I thought the more I felt it had come to me for a reason and not accidentally. I was to find out later.

It was a few days later when Tony, who was in my dream that particular night, returned from visiting his family in Mexico. I knew nothing of Tony's family; in fact, we had just recently become friends.

"How was your trip?" I asked when I saw him.

"Great," he said, and then sheepishly, "I have a message from my grandfather for you."

"Oh?" I responded uncertainly.

"He said he came to visit you. He told me to tell you he flies like a crow in the night."

A chill ran through me. My mouth dropped open in shock and surprise at hearing his words. I had not told my story to anyone other than Steve, and I could hardly believe what Tony was saying as I remembered the ghastly images.

As crazy as it seemed, I felt slightly relieved to have a partial answer to the mystery of that night. I needed more, though, so I asked Tony to tell me as much as he could.

"My grandfather lives in San Carlos Arizonaon, Mexico." he began. "One evening we sat together underneath the clear night sky. We had a small fire burning to give light. There was no wind that night — the air was still and warm, and the smoke rose upwards in small spirals. The only sounds were the crickets, crackling of the fire and my grandfather's soft yet deep voice."

Tony was interested in learning about his family roots, rituals and beliefs. His grandfather was very old and still practiced some of the ancient Toltec ways. This particular night his grandfather was teaching him an ancient Toltec practice called *Tashka-Hey*. It translates to "transmuting energy."

"The heart is projected from the sun," his grandfather said. "The heart is a flame upside-down, it is so with the beating heart. Do you understand what keeps it beating, Tony? You have confidence that it will do so tomorrow and the future days, but how much do you understand it? A tiny flame within the heart is eternal; the activity of the sacred infinite fire keeps your heart beating."

As Tony followed the abstract words, his grandfather suddenly jumped.

"He was looking right into my heart, as if he could see something there," Tony said.

"It was then without speaking about you, he told me he knew you, my friend, and he would pay you a visit. I was surprised as it was totally out of the context of what he seemed to be talking about, yet out of respect I did not question him. Grandfather told me that travel is achieved through riding upon another's dream, through a portal that is manipulated into action in the area of the third eye. My grandfather wanted to remind you of your powers. The crow was chosen so you would remember; crow is related to magic, and crow holds the possibility of creation and spiritual strength."

I felt chills run through my body again as he told me this.

"But why, Tony? What does this mean?"

"This is all I remember — maybe I was sub-consciously thinking of you at the time. You were dreaming about me after all! Maybe he saw you and recognized you. He said he knew you. Some things always remain a mystery in this life, until we learn the powers of magic."

"Your grandfather practiced magic, but what about Black Magic?" I asked, wondering about the creature's shrieking ominous words. "Do you believe in Black Magic?"

"In their ancient tradition, magic was, and still is, a part of their lives. Some of the people practiced Black Magic, using their powers to manipulate others for money or more power. I would say my gramps could be 'gray.' "

And so much of the mystery of that night was revealed to me, and much was left as mystery, too.

I have never encountered another personal entity pestering. Since that night, though, I consciously visualize a protective white light surrounding me. I think the world of Spirit holds dangers as well as rewards.

I do not equate spirituality with entities, visions and strange encounters. I, on my spiritual journey, am sensitive to energies around me. There are what we could call dark forces working in our reality, and there is no reason to think this is not so in other realities. Just like I consciously stay away from what we consider evil or bad in *this* world, I do so anywhere I go — environment is important in all realms. The darker aspects of consciousness, however they are perceived, need our love and light as a guide back to the truth, nothing is truly separate, the essence of all remains the same. As our consciousness evolves it is possible to become aware of other forms of consciousness that appear very different from our own. But ultimately we are all of the same, there is only one reality, and we are all from the one source.

Chapter Four

To Stay or Go

*Use the light that dwells within you
to regain your natural clarity of sight.*
–Lao-tzu

*I myself do nothing.
The Holy Spirit accomplishes all through me.*
–William Blake

O F ALL THE PLACES I have traveled in the world, Scotland is one of my favorites. The rugged, majestic hills rise up from the edges of the thin winding roads like towering castles. During the spring, purple heather sweeps over the slopes, softening the mountains and creating a wonderful, mystical feel. There are white beaches along the stony coastline where highland cattle, covered in long, thick hair, protecting them from the merciless winds, meander untroubled. Their large, solemn eyes watch the occasional visitor trampling in their remote habitat. It is a land of castles, stormy seas and friendly people. The landscape is wild and diverse, open to the unforgiving elements. Great stone circles and sacred places are a reminder of Scotland's ancient pagan history. It is a place of visual pleasure, exceptional discovery and enthralling adventure.

Sam and I were in England visiting my family, and so we took the opportunity to drive two hours up the coast from my small hometown of Tynemouth to visit Scotland.

We spent five days and nights exploring the wild and wonderful country. For two of those nights we stayed at the opulent Culloden Manor.

Once requisitioned by Bonnie Prince Charlie to use as his lodgings and battle headquarters prior to the fateful and final battle on Culloden Moor, Culloden House is now a handsome country manor. Standing in forty acres of elegant lawns and parkland, the tranquility and beauty of the surroundings add to the majesty of the place.

We stayed in the Garden Mansion, just to the rear of the main building, with a charming view of the quiet estate. On arriving we were warmly welcomed by our hosts and enjoyed a lovely romantic dinner in the elegant dining room. The old Scottish decor, reminiscent of its enriching past, added a wonderful ambience. The cold wind was blowing wildly outside, and the fire roared untamed in the huge fireplace. After a delicious desert, we strolled back to our room and settled down for the evening in the comfortable king bed. I soon fell into a deep slumber.

A strong, unnerving image before me wrenched me out of sleep, yet I could not move my body. Paralyzed by some unknown force, I lay bewildered by the ghastly figure. He stood ominously towering above me, a blood-splattered, spine-chilling character. Curdling blood was oozing from his wounds, dripping incredulously on my arm, burning my skin. My soul called out in anguish and heartache, a cry that matched his own. I tried to scream, urging my body to move, wanting to roll away from the gruesome red liquid that was spilling on me. But for the moment I was stuck. The hairy figure flooded me with horror and his anguish as time stood mercilessly still. He was ravaged and war torn. His large stocky figure was extremely masculine, with heavy, thick, hairy arms and legs. Dirty red and brown clothes were thrown around his shoulders like a wrap. I sensed he desperately needed help, yet I felt useless in my paralyzed state. I gathered every ounce of energy I could muster and tried to scream. "Urrgh," was all I could manage, but it was enough to pull me from the paralysis. I quickly sat up, my heart beating wildly. The image slowly faded even as I tried to hold it.

Sitting there a little startled I became conscious that the room was crowded. There were many spirits. Although I could not see them, I could easily feel and sense them. Imagine being in a crowded room, and you close your eyes, yet know there are other people about. When they are scared and not of the present time, the feeling is chilling and disturbing. The energy was highly electric. The tartan-clad man had faded, but his presence still cast a distinct supernatural feeling in the air close to me. I gingerly got out of bed and crept to the bathroom to run some water over my arm. Although my arm looked clean, the lingering heat and image of the bloody mess was still perceptible and so unpleasant on my skin, I had to get up to wash it.

I quickly returned from the bathroom, wondering what would happen next. Sam was sitting up awakened from the noises I managed to make earlier. Having some hair-raising moments himself, he turned the small lamp on. He was not seeing anything, but he could certainly sense the eerie sensations that filled the room. The hair on his arms and the back of his neck were standing on end, and his eyes were wide open, searching the room expecting to see something, the peculiar presence so strong. He looked at me expectantly. I decided to wait until morning to fill him in on the grisly details, but validated his uneasiness and whispered that I had some work to do! He kissed my cheek gently, turned off the lamp and we both lay back in bed. I began to meditate, calming myself, tuning into the vibration of the room and finding the loving essence of my heart. I began mentally calling out to any presence, telling them not to be afraid, to look for a light, to move toward that, and that everything was okay now. I felt the wonder and Divine presence fill the room.

I was following my instincts, intuition and feelings. I said a prayer for all those who died in the battle, and those who did not.

Eventually I dropped back into sleep. On awakening in the morning Sam and I held each other. We could hear the zealous wind still blowing wildly outside and see the tall trees swaying and dancing passionately through the open drapes. There are often not words to express the emotional after-effects of such an experience. I felt grateful for Sam and his loving acceptance and knowing.

We were both quite fascinated about what we had experienced the night before and so we went to visit the nearby battlefield and learnt the history of the morbid battle that had taken place so long ago.

1746, April 16th, Culloden, Scotland.

It is 11 am on a cold and misty morning. Bonnie Prince Charlie rides his fine gray gelding, attired handsomely in his tartan coat and cockaded bonnet. He carries a broadsword and loudly calls out encouraging words to his men. There are about 5,000 of them, known as Jacobites.

Not too far away, the government army, led by the Duke of Cumberland and outnumbering the Jacobites by a few thousand, prepare for battle, too, sharpening their lethal swords and knives while shrieking out for blood and killing. At last the battle begins, one of the most bloody and murderous battles in history. And only an hour later Culloden Moor is horrifyingly laden with dead and wounded.

Unsatisfied with the staggering win, Cumberland's men continue to kill, slaughtering the wounded, clubbing them to death and often obscenely mutilating their aggrieved bodies. It was not just the soldiers who suffered a horrendous death but those who had come to witness the battle — innocent bystanders, women and children, were brutally murdered without consideration. The atrocious stories of the battle and the killing that continued are notorious to this day.

I had known a little about Bonnie Prince Charlie, but none of the history of this particular battle or its whereabouts until I spent that time in Culloden House. Now it is a piece of history and a place I will undoubtedly never forget.

Sightings of Bonny Prince Charlie had often been reported in Culloden Manor, I later found out, and although I did not see him, I was sure it was the men who fought with him that I saw. As I have seen before, energy can get stuck in time, or what we perceive as time. I know this man and others were there seeking help. Hopefully they were able to hear my payers and find a guide on the other side that would show them the way home.

I know none of this was my active imagination. I have no desire to actually see this kind of thing — it just happens. I have had "people" walking through my bedroom at home, igniting tremendous, poignant emotion. Once, after an apparently horrendous car accident, I saw a group of young people pass through my room. The awful emotional upset can be disquieting. Yet I am reassured, knowing I am being of service, or Spirit would not open this up for me.

Thank goodness, though, my encounters with ghosts are not always so gruesome. It is nice to find one laughing now and again.

I was visiting Virginia to attend a meditation workshop; the room Sam and I shared was very quaint and lovely, but during the night I heard strange noises. Certain someone was in the room, I looked around uneasily, but saw nothing.

"I swear someone came through the window last night, Sam. I heard him and I could feel him walking around. Strangely I didn't see anyone, though. "If we weren't on the second floor I would have gotten up frightened, sure of an intruder." Sam had not noticed anything strange. "Maybe it was my imagination," I said.

"Probably not!" Sam replied. He was right. The following night I was able to meet the uninvited guest.

Right before I fell asleep a rather amusing face appeared at the right of my peripheral vision; he took me by surprise. He looked quite jovial and I could not help but smile myself. I wondered who he was and why he was there! The next day and evening he was there again — in fact, every time I lay on the bed he would appear. There was no verbal communication but he was often laughing. He had a triangular-shaped face with a small goatee and slight mustache, and he wore a green hat. He came and went as he pleased without any other incident. If I tried to communicate he laughed and disappeared. I had no notion of who he could be, but a few days later my questions were answered when I related the incidents to one of our facilitators.

"What room are you in?" Bob asked. When I replied, he said, "Ah, that would be the colonel!"

"The colonel?" I asked, surprised that he seemed to know him so well.

"Yes, he's been there some time. We don't usually tell anyone. Occasionally people see him, and he seems very friendly. I've met him a couple of times, and he won't talk to me either. He seems to have no intention of moving on, so we just leave him alone."

"Okay," I said. Sam and I looked at each other and shrugged our shoulders. "So what's new!"

Chapter Five

Gifts
of the
Animal Kingdom

*My arms turned into wings; I felt their power and lightness
as they gracefully glided through the wind.
My face transformed; I felt a dense strong beak,
and from my new wise eyes I could see the earth below.
I was irrefutably strong and mighty
as I soared through the infinite sky,
Eagle in my domain.*
–Julie Yau

*T*HERE IS AN ASPECT OF MYSELF that is like a wild cat. I love and appreciate the gracefulness of the animal, and I covet its flexible and relaxed body. I find it delightful to stretch and roll, unwinding my body outside on the rocks or inside beside a warm crackling fire. I enjoy time alone, wandering through canyons, and I love to be touched but never held with constraint, or I will twist and turn and escape the unwelcome clutches. You have to wait until I come to you, or you must sense that I trust you and then I will allow you to approach. But most of all I love to run and feel the sovereignty of my strength and independence. This is myself as a panther.

My relationship to the cat is not just a physical one but mystical, too. My power animal is the sleek and powerful panther. I sense its presence and prowess as it watches over me when I journey to the lower world. The lower world is a place one can journey to in a non-ordinary state of consciousness to acquire power and knowledge from ordinarily hidden dimensions of reality. The experiences can be likened to lucid dreams in which one controls and directs the adventure. I run with panther when I am there, and we sit together in reverence, acknowledging the sacredness of our time together. I sometimes catch a glimpse of her in this reality when I wistfully watch the hypnotic ocean and admire the perfection of nature. She sits close, upright and majestic; lately I saw a diamond necklace elegantly clasped around her neck. I smiled, elatedly wondering what the significance and symbology of her presence was. The periphery vision reveals the hidden dimensions; much can be unveiled through its unfiltered perception.

The lower world is a place of animals and nature. I use visualization and drumming to take me there, and once there I allow the magic to unfold around me. The panther is often waiting there for me. I first met panther many years ago, before I knew of shamanic rituals and journeys to the upper and lower realms. It came in a dream that was no less real than the waking state.

> *My physical body was sleeping, but I was running on the canyon rocks, my body feeling strong and supple. I could leap and glide from rock to rock without effort. I could sense the joy of freedom and the lightness of body that my powerful muscles gave as my legs stretched and leapt with ease and grace. To my left side ran a large black cat, a panther, beautiful with awesome orange eyes. Its glossy coat was shimmering in the moonlight as its muscles rippled in slow motion with its graceful movements. For a while I was in awe of this exquisite creature — its vigilance, auspicious independence and mystical prowess. Then I could sense and*

see my own feet. Large black paws. I knew I was panther, too. We ran with synchronistic strides, elegant black beasts exuberantly running together through the night. I was fearless and passionate. Wild with strong animal impulses, sensations and power, I fully merged with the instincts of an untamed cat.

I woke from my sleep, my heart pounding with excitement and my forehead covered in beads of sweet sweat, and I knew it was more than a dream I had just experienced. My body was still holding a slight sensation of the physical representation of a panther, and I reveled in the preciousness of it. In ancient Shamanic traditions around the world it is not so unusual for a Shaman to metamorphose into the form of their guardian power animal. I was riveted to have undergone such a rapturous and sacrosanct evening.

A few months later I lay sleeping when something disturbed me and woke me from my deep slumber. I opened my eyes and was caught by surprise by a large black panther sitting on the table a few feet from the bed. In shock I began to slowly sit up as we looked into each others' eyes, and for a moment I was held by its silence and stealth, magnetized by the brilliance and intensity of the experience. Before I had time to further react its hind legs stretched and with one swift movement it jumped toward me. I instinctively braced myself for the impact, tensing my body and holding my breath in fear. In one swift moment it gracefully merged with me, softly disappearing inside me. Ecstatic and slightly disorientated, I sat there, my breath rapid, and I began to gently vibrate. Captivated by the spine-tingling sensations that followed, I sat in wonder while I listened to the quiet noises of the night, the wind blowing, an owl hooting and crickets singing. I acknowledged my connection to the panther, curious about the archaic meaning it signified.

I look forward to falling asleep, never knowing what the night might bring. When I go beyond the sleeping state to explore realms of my own consciousness, I return with gifts and insights which enhance my waking state.

Intrigued, I explored the myth and legend of the Black Panther and was not surprised to see how intimately we are connected.

I found my lesson in this life of overcoming negative and self-destructive tendencies is in alignment with this archetypal nature of the panther. I can learn from the stories of old, seeing myself reflected in the great legends and the path to wholeness. I know the panther is my guardian as well as my symbol for rebirth, claiming my own feminine power and a sign of awakening of my kundalini energy.

Kundalini is a very potent form of pranic or cosmic energy, said to lie dormant at the base of our spine. Kundalini is no less than a healing force when allowed to run its course, bringing us direct spiritual illumination and spiritual evolution. The gift of the panther as my power animal foretold of the kundalini awakenings that were soon to come, so in a way I was prepared for the surprising emergence of energies that would again take me to a higher level of awareness. The stories will come later in the book.

The phenomenon of shape-shifting is extraordinary. To transcend the imagination and embrace a unique awareness through metamorphosis is exquisite. It is uniquely freeing as the ordinary mind surpasses its boundaries and realizes its potential to create an experience that is authentic at a different level of reality.

As I sat in meditation I began to feel a delightful energy filling my body. It was gentle and pure and I began to move slowly and rhythmically to the soft music that was playing in the background. My mind was quiet and I was just allowing myself to be as I focused intently on my breath. My arms began floating softly without effort, the energy itself moving them until my whole body joined the elegant dance. I danced slowly, rhythmically and trance-like, staying with my breath and not letting the lightness of my body or any thoughts distract me. I eventually dropped softly to my knees with my arms behind me and the intoxicating transformation began.

My arms began a delicate metamorphosis. A molecular shifting spiraled through me until the great wings of an eagle spun outward from my back. The awesome cosmic energy that had filled my body continued to allow me to transform, and with my eyes gently closed I experienced my whole body transform into the powerful bird. I knew the greatness and lightness of my new-found wings as they graciously glided through the wind. My face transformed, I felt a dense, strong beak, and from my new eyes I could see the beautiful Earth below. I was irrefutably strong and mighty. As I soared through the infinite sky I was eagle in his domain.

It is possible to embody any form as we embody this natural cosmic energy. The feminine creative aspect of the Godhead fills us, or it can take us on its own journey. It is an experience of the soul, the individualized spirit being free, expressing itself in our realm. It was an inward journey of course; anyone witnessing me would have seen me moving gently, my arms spread out like wings, but the experience of being the eagle was genuine. Cosmic energy is the missing dynamic between body and spirit, matter and consciousness. It is ever-present, but often blocked by the ego from the surface of our consciousness. As it flows through me I begin to realize the true nature of the Self, infinite and absolute. Archetypal energy, too, I sense working from within and without, connecting me with the collective unconscious, filling and allowing me to experience influences and aspects of other realms. I gain an inner mobility as I become a vessel for energy, and the veil between the unconscious and conscious becomes thinner. I experience grace, authenticity and an intense aliveness, like a crystal dazzling as the sun strikes it at dawn.

The joys of these experiences are usually limited to myself, yet it is possible to touch others as the potential of the energy goes beyond the personal.

I was part of a trio working with counseling skills. Something was troubling me, though, as I had just observed my soon-to-be counselor discuss the downward spiraling of his life. He shared his misery and hopelessness without any aspiration to change. In fact, the images of his conversation conveyed to me a large black hole, which I began to see clearly with my inner vision, that continued to expand, sucking in all the help that his counselor offered him and creating an even graver mood. He then described these images to be his feelings — his black hole getting bigger and darker. As I took the turn to be the client I looked inward to see what was present for me. The truth was that I was feeling peaceful and joyous, yet susceptible at the awful account of depression from my counselor. As I looked into his eyes I received no encouragement. I silently repeated the words, "I love you, I love you," over and over again, directing the energy to my counselor. As I sat still with my eyes closed, aware of my heart and the loving energy that was filling it, the sensation expanded outward reaching my whole body. A familiar impression of lightness subtly excited me as my body began to gently vibrate. After a short while I opened my eyes. "I need to move, to dance," I said smiling. My two partners looked at me curiously. We stood up and I could feel the luminous energy craving expression. My arms light and floating, it was not an animal this time that my body felt a shift into but a tiny dancing fairy. I could sense the buoyancy and gentleness of my whole body slowly moving, up on my toes, whimsically dancing in slow, graceful movements, the mystery of the subtle dimensions enchanting myself as well as the two onlookers. Fully immersed in my experience I allowed the magic to unfold. The distinguishing characteristics of my own body started to dissolve. No longer limited by my ordinary mind I became the vessel for Spirit. I could feel loving, healing energy coursing through my arms. I was the medium for this goddess fairy to exist.

I knew this was a healing experience; there was no doubt, and it was not for me but for my counselor. I was truly merged with cosmic energy that floated out to those watching me. I saw their faces transform, their eyes beginning to glisten in wonder and delight. They sensed this was magical, beyond the ordinary and they began to laugh enjoying the merriment of the unusual experience. The three of us sat down again, reveling in the undeniable mystery of what was taking place. As my counselor brought forward his enjoyment he also made reference to his hopelessness. My hand lifted, guided still by the wonderful energy. What happened next was truly exquisite. I spontaneously sprinkled him with fairy dust. Invisible silver brilliance showered us with love.

"You are no longer troubled, no longer hopeless and depressed." I laughed delightedly. "It's not possible to resist the power of fairy dust."

We laughed and laughed as I continued to sprinkle him. It was an almost ludicrous scene and yet it was magical. His protests dissolved into laughter and joy, and an amazing discovery took place. To him the laughter was a miracle; it had been such a long time since he had felt even remotely happy. Seeing Spirit move through me and touch him was undeniable and forceful enough to shift the energy dynamics of his life.

To allow myself to work with the mysteries of the power of love is to me a miraculous gift as I see not only how it fills me with joy but how it can profoundly touch others. Lightness of heart is surely a path to freedom, and the creative expression of energy can help us to transcend limiting beliefs and patterns that hold us back from who we truly are.

One path in which to experience this is through certain meditation techniques. Holding an intention to allow yourself to be filled with Spirit, allow the luminous energy to tantalize your imagination and experience the gifts of Spirit.

Chapter Six

Sai *Baba*

Where there is Faith, there is Love;
Where there is Love, there is Peace;
Where there is Peace, there is Truth;
Where there is Truth, there is Bliss;
Where there is Bliss there is God.
–Sai Baba

I WOKE UP BEFORE DAWN, stretched happily from under my sleeping bag, then unzipped the flimsy canvas door of my tent. The air was cool outside, but effervescent and refreshing as my head peaked out into the early morning, pulling the vitality and energy into my lungs. I dressed in warm clothes — several layers so I could peel them off as the morning warmed. I excitedly crawled out of the tent to meet the day and pulled on my hiking boots. The sky was a light indigo and I knew I had only a short time before the sun rose. My destination was the top of a small hill, a handsome vantage point to observe the mighty sunrise and see the land light up with a fiery glow. I drank some cold water, splashed it on my face and began to hastily walk through the desert brush. I was careful to place my feet on the plain ground and not disturb the growth. In twenty minutes I reached the top of the mound, as the sun was beginning to cheerfully peek above the low mountains in the distance. I took a deep breath, filling my body with the beauty and power of a new day as it gloriously emerged. Birds singing and dancing in the clear sky around me, I was gleefully smiling and enjoying each moment. Nature is the medicine for my heart and soul. I am constantly amazed at her newness and perfection. Her splendid, inescapable creativity and awesome expressions nourish me. I stamped my feet on the ground, celebrating my being there, then turned and swiftly ran down the hill, laughing as the wind caught my hair and I feeling like a gazelle, light limbed and free.

I was in Sedona, Arizona for a few days of hiking, and this day was to bring not only the wonders of nature, but the first of a sequence of synchronistic events that guided me to the distant land of India.

When I arrived back at my campsite, I filled a small pack for the day and drove the short distance to town. I went to the Coffee Roasters, my favorite café for breakfast, before venturing out for a full day's hike. I loved the warm ambience of locals and strangers gathering for the morning ritual of coffee and tea. I found a comfortable chair so I could see outside to the lovely red rocks. I watched the transient shadows slowly rising and fading as the hot, morning desert sun rose brilliantly above them. I slowly and deliberately ate my breakfast. I looked forward to hiking and exploring on the mountains, connecting with nature and the wonders of the outdoors. This particular morning a friend whom I had met many years before stopped by to say hello. I smiled cheerfully; it was lovely to see him. Tain was a local and I always enjoyed his company and listening to his fascinating stories. He sat down and we chatted for a while. Having just returned from India, he was excited to tell me about Sai Baba, an Avatar whom he had seen, and had been overwhelmed with his extraordinariness. An Avatar, he told me is an incarnation of God who comes to this Earth in human form, and in spite of the body he assumes, he is not limited by the usual human boundaries of time and space. He is ever-present and ubiquitous.

I listened attentively.

"Sai Baba's love and power spreads throughout the world and humanity. He's like a modern-day Jesus Christ in India," he told me matter-of-factly. "Thousands of people gather to see him every day for Darshan, to receive his grace just by being in his presence. He performs miracles, manifesting objects to give to his devotees and sacred ash for healing; daily miracles happen. It's amazing."

Tain became more excited as he revealed his story and his enthusiasm really got me interested. I wondered about what he said, but I realized I knew very little about this part of the world — Avatars and Gurus — yet I found myself becoming quite intrigued. As he eagerly talked on, my attention was drawn to his right to a rather unusual sight. An apparition had appeared next to him. An oval luminescent light, about the height of a small man, was hovering innocently. An ethereal bystander was watching over us. A warm sensation filled my body as I took in the ghostly figure. There was no relevant explanation for what I was seeing and Tain seemed unaware, and if there was a look of puzzlement on my face, he probably attributed it to his story-telling. The moment had a feel of sacredness as I absorbed the vision and I continued to sit and listen without divulging the curious sight. Tain carried on with his story excitedly.

"Sai Baba will call to people if you're meant to go and see him. He will send a sign, not in a formal way, of course — more like a dream or something!"

A shiver ran through my body as he said this, and as he spoke I wondered if this radiant entity was the omnipresent Sai Baba, his mystical appearance a calling for me. I really didn't know, but my interest was certainly piqued.

"How does one go about seeing him?" I asked as the luminescent figure began to slowly fade.

"Oh, it's easy. If you're meant to go, you will. Once you're in India everyone knows of him. His picture seemed to be everywhere I looked."

It all sounded very intriguing, and the luminous vision quite roused my curiosity. Eventually I bid Tain farewell and I ventured out into the hills, thoughts of India and Avatars fading from my mind as I became absorbed in the beauty of the rocks, the plants and the quiet. I didn't think much more of the event until a couple of months later.

I was traveling quite a bit at the time, attending various seminars and workshops on body, mind and Spirit. During a class in Canada I overheard one of the girls talk about her recent trip to India. My attention was drawn and I keenly began to listen. She had with her some vibhuti, the sacred ash that Sai Baba magically manifests, pulling it from the air about him. She noticed my curiosity and offered me some, placing a pinch on my forehead. I did not have a strong reaction other than knowing this was a significant moment, but something inside me stirred restlessly. My interest in this man grew. Sai Baba manifests this sacred ash, and visitors and devotees are welcome to take some before they leave the ashram. There are little packets wrapped up for this purpose. In Sai Baba's first incarnation, of which he will have three, he was known as Sai Baba of Shirdi. This Hatha Yogi continuously burnt a fire and would distribute the ash to his devotees for cures to illness and for inner transformation. The ash he gives in this lifetime may be symbolic, or maybe it is used for healing, too.

I was probably more interested than I let myself believe. I had never been drawn to Gurus and was not quite sure about the probability of an Avatar. Looking back now, after meeting many extraordinary spiritual teachers, I am awake to the knowledge that these enlightened beings walk so purely and brightly amongst us. As I love to travel and adventure I began to play a game with myself.

"Okay," I thought. "If Sai Baba is brought to my attention again soon, that will be three times. I'll take it as a sign that I should go to India and see him."

Well, it was not much later that Sam and I were attending a workshop given by Aminah Rahmeen, Ph.D., the founder of Process Acupressure and author of *Soul Return*, at the Esalen Institute in Big Sur, California. At lunchtime we sat with Aminah and her husband, Fritz Smith. India came up in our conversation, and Aminah told us that one of her spiritual teachers is Sai Baba. She makes the pilgrimage to India each year to visit his ashram. Sai Baba has been a powerful and wonderful influence in her life, and both she and Fritz told us some intriguing stories about him.

So that was three times, and I knew then I was going to see Sai Baba. I felt a synchronistic tapestry had been woven as a calling for me to go. I knew more events would unfold soon, and I would be discovering the secrets and mysticism of India. I intentionally opened up to a journey of fun and learning. And so it came about in the most astonishing way.

Not long after our first meeting with Aminah and Fritz, Sam and I decided to attend one of Fritz's classes on Zero Balancing. Zero Balancing is a hands-on technique that evaluates and balances the relationship between energy and structure. Fritz is the founder of this profound and insightful work. One evening after class Fritz invited Sam and me to dinner. Aminah joined us and she shared some very exciting news.

A trip to India was in the making. Both Fritz and Aminah would be teaching a class in Bangalore. The class would

combine both of their practices and afterward, for those who
were interested, a trip to Sai Baba's Ashram. I was overjoyed at
hearing the news and Sam and I immediately indicated our
interest to join the class. Specific plans had not been arranged,
but I felt inside that this trip would happen and I would be on
my way to India to see Sai Baba within the next year.

As if that were not enough, I had a very special encounter
with Sai Baba before I went. Our friendship with Aminah and
Fritz had grown and we were visiting their lovely home.
Aminah had graciously allowed me to give her some bodywork
I was practicing. She lay on the massage table and I sat at the
head placing my hands on her shoulders. We were in her living
room, and I had admired the pictures of Sai Baba adorning the
fireplace and desk when we arrived. Concentrating on Aminah
and my hands, I was taken completely by surprise when from
my peripheral vision Sai Baba rose out of his picture. A huge,
three-dimensional image of him appeared and captivated me.
He grew to quite a size before magically disappearing again. It
was so extraordinary and clear, I was shocked. Here again was
the warming presence of Sai Baba. This time I could have no
doubt it was him. The beautiful expanding image of him was
not the most exciting thing; it was the warming fluid sensation
of divine love that accompanied it. My heart was suddenly
flung open as the depth of love ricocheted around my body. The
sweet divine presence sizzled through me. My hands were still
placed on Aminah's shoulders, and without knowing what I
had just seen she sweetly whispered, "Sai Baba is here."

I felt the deep love of devotion from Aminah and the
unconditional love of Sai Baba sweep through us. The intensity
was convincing. I thought right then I would let go of any
expectations of Sai Baba. I did not need anything else. Feeling
this divine love was nourishing for my soul. The essence of who

I am sensed Sai Baba as it seeped into me like perfect, sweet truth. I sat profoundly grateful for the fact I was going to India with the possibility he would be at the Ashram.

A year later when I arrived in Bangalore I saw a large unframed picture of Sai Baba plastered to a wall in the airport, his smiling face greeting me warmly. At 3 AM, the air was cool but humid. From high above the full moon flooded an illuminating light, casting shadows and creating an eerie glow to the new surroundings. Besieged with the strange sights and pungent aromas of the new environment, I readily took in the setting and solemn ambience of the unique outer city as we rode in a taxi to the hotel. Silently driving through the moonlit, ramshackle towns, as if in a dream, I watched the distinctive scenes unfold before me. People were sleeping next to each other on the streets, right out in the open or under wobbly, make-shift roofs of corrugated iron. Here and there people were awake, sitting around small fires, boiling water or cooking some food, perhaps. The mood felt somber as I watched the people resigned to the poverty that surrounded them, and my heart went out to them. Children and elderly alike huddled close to one another or sat utterly alone in the shadows. Their sober eyes followed me as we drove by, and strangely I felt connected, with a sense of familiarity and reverence in the moment. Yet I was also a transient observer, passing silently through the scenes of their life, like a fleeting shadow. Periodically wondering what their lives were like, I absorbed the austerity, dubious that I would ever really know.

As we neared the city center the buildings became larger and more modern. I could have been in a city anywhere in the world. Pulling up at the plush-looking hotel, we were pleasantly surprised. Sam and I checked in and grabbed a few hours of sleep. When we woke up we excitedly dressed and ventured out into the city with a spirit of adventure.

Bangalore is the capital of Karnakata State in Southeast India; it is known for its ancient temples and its flamboyant palaces as well as being one of the fastest growing cosmopolitan cities in India, often called the "Silicon Valley of India." The city is a conglomeration of poverty and riches, inundated with smog, animals, heavy traffic and sporadic parks so one can try to escape the chronic noise and pollution. Lal Bagh Park was especially beautiful with 240 acres of sculpted gardens. Myriad flower beds and a lovely lake resonated the subtle magnetism of nature's beautiful love. Sam and I spent hours wandering around, enjoying the botanical gardens and peaceful ambience of the park, far away from the chaos of the city streets.

I enjoyed the city, too, amused by the fast pace and cheery aggressiveness of the people. We found ourselves being hustled into old rickshaws and hastily driven to stores we had no desire to visit. Trying on and buying oversized clothes; we were assured they were perfect, and we humorously realized that was the only size available. "Look," one persuasive shopkeeper said unwaveringly, "I wear that size, very good." He was twice the size of Sam, but that did not deter his marketing. Our maxim was "surrender," and with lightheartedness we enjoyed the pandemonium and innovative entrepreneurs. The week was full and invigorating in many ways. The workshop was a tonic for the heart and soul; students from five different countries brought a cultural diversity to the class I had not experienced before. Respect of different cultures brought us to a deeper level of communication and admiration for one another.

Once the workshop came to an end, choosing not to stay in Bangalore a moment longer than necessary, Sam and I left immediately for Puttaparthy, the home of Sai Baba's Ashram.

The journey took a few hair-raising hours on a winding, rugged and dusty road. Our native driver had a perverse death wish I did not want to be part of. Refusing to move over for any oncoming traffic on the very thin road he played chicken with every oncoming vehicle. He suddenly lost all capability to understand English, and my not-so-polite words to slow down were to no avail. I sustained myself with deep breaths and clutching tightly to Sam's hand. There were moments of gratification on the treacherous ride. To glimpse the land, its people and a culture like no other, was a blessing. There were parched rivers waiting patiently for rain. Men of all ages sat solemnly under bare trees, watching with bright eyes, while women carried heavy loads, dressed so cheerfully, along the dusty roads. Eventually we arrived safe and sound at our very simple hotel, albeit a little shaken and tense. The temperamental air conditioning was a great blessing, along with warm water so we could cleanse ourselves from sticky perspiration after the arduous drive. Excitedly we changed into appropriate clothing. I wore a light-colored sari and Sam dressed in a simple white outfit like most of the men do.

Our first Darshan was to begin at 2:30 PM. We walked leisurely to the ashram, called Prasanthi Nilayam, the Abode of Peace. The village felt alive and animated as we strolled along the dirt road. Full of activity and noise, the streets were lined with small shops selling everything from cookies to luggage. Colorful and cheerful the people seemed, yet looking closer I could see the struggle on faces lined with hardships that we in the West rarely have to endure. As I walked I began to notice a warming sensation in the air, the gentle vibrations of divine love of Sai Baba.

Inside the ashram were beautiful gardens and a breathtaking temple within the center of the main structure. It sat majestically, painted the gentle colors of pink, yellow and baby blue. Huge golden lions graced the end of an awesome hall where I would soon be graced by Sai Baba's presence. Tremors of excitement were flowing through me as the realization struck me — I was about to see Sai Baba. My mind sang, as gentle waves of gratitude tenderly touched my heart. Sam and I parted, as the custom calls for the men and women to be separated. I read it is important here because of the energy currents that run between the opposite sexes. As we sit so close to each other in meditation, it is better to not have that distraction. I joined the moving crowd of women, feeling a part of a pilgrimage, walking quickly toward our side of the great hall.

Thousands of us sat exceedingly close together and waited patiently in the sweltering heat. With our legs crossed and knees and elbows sticking rudely into each other, we endured the soaring temperature. The first couple of days I looked around, absorbing the unique environment and culture which is exclusive to Indian ashrams. I then used my time more appropriately, and sat in meditation, prayer or reading, using the opportunity to gain control of my mind and develop a more meditative attitude. After an hour or so of sitting in tightly packed rows, a ticket number was given to the head of each line. A flurry of excitement ran through us. The lines with the lowest numbers get to enter the prayer hall first, therefore having a seat hopefully closer to where Sai Baba would walk. This process is interesting. The Indian ladies were so anxious to get inside they tried to jump lines, grab tickets, push ahead and get in front of anyone they could. This was curiously touching, their incredible desire to be close to Sai Baba reflecting love and devotion. There were ladies called Sea Dal Volunteers, recognizable by their bright orange scarves and persuasive attitudes, directing the crowds, and overall everything was quite orderly.

After an hour or so the gate was opened and we filed silently and quickly into the temple. The women could barely help themselves from running, so excited and eager. Everyone wanted to be in the front row where Sai Baba would walk by, but only a few would get that opportunity. Bare feet ran across the stone floor. Bright emerald and yellow saris flowed gracefully, the heat momentarily forgotten. We all found a space to sit on the floor, feeling closer to heaven, and again began to patiently wait.

Soft, celestial music began to play. All eyes turned excitedly to the gate where Sai Baba gracefully entered. I was struck with wonder at his divine presence, and with a feeling of tenderness and a desire to reach out and embrace him. My heart rejoiced with love as I watched him walk slowly into the temple. He was smaller than I imagined, with a crown of unique, dark, curly hair. The energy that emanated from him was overwhelming. He moved with poise, dressed in a long, bright orange robe, making gentle expressive hand gestures, occasionally stopping to quietly say a few words to the adoring people close by him, or to accept a heartfelt letter. I remember thinking just how beautiful he was. Duly humbled, never before had I felt the desire to bow down, to place my forehead on the ground in respect. The feeling being so strong, my hands went to my heart and my eyes lowered as I bowed my head. As my mind emptied of thought I floated in the grace that filled the air. Aware only of the stillness of love and the warmth of my tears as they rolled gently down my cheeks, I stumbled upon bliss.

Slowly Sai Baba walked around the hall. He stopped by someone close to me and I saw the fine grey ash, or vibhuti, fall miraculously from his hand into the palm of an excited young women. Later I witnessed jewelry being magically manifested from the air as generous gifts to distinguished visitors. Then I tasted the sweet, sticky foods that are brought into existence with a slight sweep of his hand — an incredible feat and phenomenal accomplishment. Yet what I witnessed did not epitomize the essence of Sai Baba. He showed us the potential of our own selves, which still lies dormant in the depths of our true beings. The enchantment was the pure energy of love that sprang forth from this beloved man. Sai Baba took about twenty minutes to walk through the hall and then entered one of the back meditation rooms. The melodious tunes of the Bajans, devotional songs, rang out through the temple as people sang in praise. Not knowing the words I allowed the resonance to lovingly permeate my heart. After thirty minutes of glorious singing, silence fell. Sai Baba walked by us once again, his presence leaving a glow like a brilliant sunset. On his departure we were free to leave for the day. This time was spent in quiet reflection and eating a light dinner before falling into a welcome sleep.

The next Darshan was early the next morning. It was quiet and peaceful outside at 4 AM. The air felt fresh and clean after the night's heavy tropical rain. The velvety black sky was graced with luminous stars and a slither of orange moon enhanced the perfectly painted picture.

"How faithful the moon is," I thought tenderly. "Night after night, always present, showing itself in its full glory, or gracing the sky with the slightest part of itself." There were a few people meandering about, setting up vending stalls or on their way to Darshan. A huge pig was clumsily rummaging amongst the garbage on the street, inadvertently helping to clean it up for the new day. I felt wonderful and tranquil. Dawn was magical, a time between the worlds. With so many people sleeping, and many meditating, fewer thoughts filled the air. At the ashram the same procedure as the afternoon before was followed. As I sat in stillness under the indigo sky, Omkar began; this is the chanting of the sacred syllable "Om" twenty-one times. The sound was stirring and emotive. It vibrated powerfully into my core, and as I chanted I felt the resonance with five thousand others. Each morning these were very intoxicating moments.

And so the week went, Darshan twice a day, each one precious, full of love, gratitude and enigmatic opportunities to be with myself.

One of the most enchanting moments for me was when Sai Baba sang. The soft, captivating music of his voice thrilled and electrified, like a thousand angels filling the air as the beautiful sounds resonated through me and transported me to a place of exquisite love. Tears again rolling down my cheeks, I knew I was present with a being who knew who he was, a realized being whose purpose is to spread love around the world, encouraging us all to realize who we truly are.

Patience grew as I sat in pensive mood at the ashram. There were so many hours of sitting, with body odors and body parts infusing my personal space as we lingered in the barely tolerant heat. Usually easy going and relaxed, one particularly uncomfortable day I sat sweating profusely, my mind and body moaning and complaining with the unwieldy surroundings. My skin was burning from the needling mosquitoes which were greedily feasting on my hands and face. I seriously began to question my sanity. This day had felt particularly wretched, as unpleasant pungent aromas saturated the humid air about me. Everyone seemed to be sneezing and coughing in my direction and my body was cramping unmercifully in the small space I occupied. I took a sorrowful breath, feeling somewhat pitiful. A moment later the delightful smell of magnolias filled my nostrils, the sweetness beyond pleasure, as a small white feather floated down and landed elegantly on my lap. Like a soft sweet kiss from heaven its fragile appearance elevated my spirit. I took in its delicate softness, purity and simplicity. I laughed in sheer joy as I was brought gracefully back into the moment. I felt all the blessings, saw the beauty, and thought to myself, "I am blessed to be in such a rapturous place. I could be here forever and ever and I know it will become more glorious still." I stayed at the temple longer that day, dwelling in the exquisiteness. With a scarf draped over my hands and face to deter the mosquitoes, even the heat could not disturb the joyous love I felt.

Such a powerful being as Sai Baba knows what we are thinking, what we need to learn and what will be for our highest good. There is no doubt for me when he appears in my dreams that there is a deep teaching. Shortly after I returned home I had two dreams that affected me quite intensely.

> *I was on the beach with a few other people. Sai Baba was there and he allowed me to have my picture taken with him. He then held out his hand and lovingly encouraged me to come into the ocean. I knew the ocean represented absolute freedom, a merging back into the original source, yet as I ran toward the gentle waves and the promise of illumination I stopped to take off my diamond earrings. I did not want to lose them, thinking of Sam who had given them to me. Sai Baba stood immersed in the glistening waters watching me, and I saw myself and the lesson I was learning.*

The dream faded and I woke, feeling disturbed that I had not awakened by merging into the oceanic bliss that beckoned, yet I knew there was no judgment from Sai Baba and I was able to have compassion for myself and learn. I had received a great teaching about my own self-imposed limitations — my attachment to things, people and what I imagine they represent. There is surprising potency and freedom in the detachment and relinquishing of desires. As the energy of attachment is released I gain back my personal power. I live more fully in the moment experiencing the abundance of life itself, moving closer to that ocean of absolute freedom.

I longed to return to India, to go back to the ashram and see Sai Baba. I felt such a deep love for this enlightened being and a desire to be close to him and his teachings, but my schedule did not allow for another trip. At times my heart ached — of course my yearning and love were heard. And as Sai Baba said, *"No person can dream of Swami unless Swami Himself desires it so."* I received another wonderful dream:

> *I am in the ashram anxiously waiting for Sai Baba to appear. When he does he is walking with a woman holding a child. They walk up to me and I am thrilled to be seen. I watch the woman lovingly holding the child and smiling at me, then they slowly walk away. Sai Baba remains and I feel my heart racing, unsure what to do; he reaches out his hand and touches the top of my head and I realize I am to bow down and touch his feet. This is the greatest honor. I bow my head down to the ground. My hands reach out and touch his feet and the enormity of the heat surprises me. My hands burn as the incredible warmth begins to flood through my body.*

I woke up with tears pouring gratefully from my eyes; my humble heart blossomed with respect and awe to receive such blessing as to touch the lotus feet of Sri Sathya Sai Baba. The sun shone brighter that day than it ever had before, warm and serene. My mind was awakening like a golden daffodil on a spring morning. I remembered Sai Baba's words, reminding me of the connection of us all.

"You are the star and least little blade of grass.
You shine as dew on the petal of the rose; you swing from star to star; you are part and parcel of all this manifestation."

Chapter Seven

Freedom
through
Flying

No pessimist ever discovered the secrets of the stars,
or sailed to an uncharted land,
or opened a new heaven to the human spirit.
–Helen Keller

The most beautiful thing we can experience is the mysterious.
–Albert Einstein

*I*T WAS THE FIRST MORNING in my new apartment on Balboa Island. I was twenty-one. I woke up feeling wonderful; the sense of freedom swelling in me, I imagined was like that of an angel with newfound wings. During the night I had lifted up from my bed and body and found myself above the houses, looking down over the island. I was flying. The triggering events of my night's escapade were the dynamic expressions of freedom I was experiencing in life at that time. A new job, a new car and my own apartment for the first time in the States, gave me a delectable sense of autonomy. I was feeling swanky and chic, independent and ready to take on the world. The feelings of happiness still make me laugh affectionately as I recall the lightness of being. Oh, the innocence and fearlessness as I euphorically flew around the twilight sky like a kingfisher encircling its haven. Around and around I soared, as I discovered flight in the eternal sky, delighted with the fantastic sense of freedom I was experiencing. I flew past tall trees from above, the surrounding water, calm and tranquil in the bay, with the moon casting many shadows on its glittering surface. I loved how the little bridge to the mainland looked quaint, quiet and magical in the early hours. Suddenly I awoke with a slight start in my bed. My eyes opened wide as warm and rejuvenating sensations tingled through my body.

"Wow," I thought. "That was incredible." I knew then I had been out of my body.

My spirit had been joyously celebrating its accomplishment of the simple phases of my life as Julie that were so empowering. The joy could not be bottled up in my body; it had to be free to really express the triumph, and how I did! Flying and swooping without a care in the world. I now had an exquisite memory to cherish; it was my first out-of-body experience.

Other OBE's that I encountered were additionally exciting, opening up new possibilities of connection to a whole, rather than an individual self, in other realms of existence within our universe. Here is one such incidence.

During the night I find myself floating up out of my body; this is not so unusual anymore. I move toward the bedroom wall, and quite calmly I think, "Am I going to hit the wall and hurt myself?" Not taking into account that it is the middle of the night or that I am not walking but floating, there is no rationality in my thinking. As I come to the wall I move right through it, like a ghost free to move through solid matter, and I find myself moving outward into the night at a great speed. My last recollection is usually of the starry vastness of space. The curtain is usually drawn here. My soul's journey into unknown realms is to nourish itself from the source and then return before I awake in the morning to continue the weird and wonderful human experience.

It is not actually necessary for our soul to leave the body to nourish itself, for everything is within. My journeys or meditations that are directed inward where I experience the vastness of space and the true awareness of Self are the most illuminating and revealing. True awareness is experienced every night on falling asleep as we enter deep, dreamless sleep, but we rarely remember, oblivious to the caring scheme of Spirit. Like a death, we have completely surrendered. Our ordinary mind and ego becomes silent and we are absorbed into vast space and awareness of who we truly are. Few eternal wanderers recall, the kings of emptiness are living through the gates of life and death, nothing kept from their infinite knowledge.

The energy that leaves the physical is called the astral body; it is made up of light and much higher vibration, hence its ability to move through matter. There are obviously fewer limitations for the astral body; time, distance and thought do not have the same significance as in the physical realm. Thought is the vehicle in which we travel; think of a location, the next moment the astral body is there, quicker than the kingfisher. It is a striking and magical affair.

A revealing and exhilarating out-of-body experience happened once while I was awake.

I was in a car on the way to Sedona, Arizona, driving through the dry desert and high mountains with two friends. I loved to see the tall saguaro cacti that stand like statues, sparsely scattered over the parched, rocky landscape, with soft white flowers blooming delicately at the tips of their outspread arms. Nature reflected to me perfectly the essence of fragility and strength. The bare, rugged mountains all around were beautiful in their own commanding way, fearlessly standing in the unforgiving heat, their only company tumbleweeds hastily blowing by, tormented by hot desert winds. We approached Sedona from the south, coming down the mountain through an old mining town called Jerome. As we left this quaint, artsy town I glimpsed our destination for the first time. I was immediately struck by the beauty of the red rocks in the distance, my eyes merrily dancing with the thrill of the unusual tapestry of terrestrial colors.

The next moment I was fantastically flying through the air toward the magnificent rocks. There was no time to think — I was enveloped in mystery and the enigma, amazingly real and exquisite.

Almost instantly I was on a colorful red rock, lying face down, aware of the shape of my body and sensing its lightness. I could not see my body, but it felt like my arms were spread out wide, and I was looking to the left, my right cheek softly touching the rock surface. An awesome feeling of connection and communication with the rock was present. Gently sinking down into the rock I turned my head to the right. My body was immersed in the rock's beauty. It was alive, and I could sense its consciousness. I realized I had merged with nature and was receiving a warm and loving embrace. I became one with the rock. I knew we were separate, yet there was no separation of consciousness that is inherent in all things.

The next moment I was flying back through the air as I heard my friends speaking, and my body jerked as I reentered it at great speed.

I was sitting in the center of the back seat of the car as all this happened, looking excitedly at the view through the front window. Seeing me through the rear-view mirror, Steve watched me for a while as I became absolutely still. Not able to tell if I was breathing, he said to John, "She's not asleep; her eyes are open." It was when they spoke that I remember being pulled back to my body.

That event excited and moved me deeply, and certainly piqued my curiosity about how it had happened. It felt as if the deeper essence of who I am, overwhelmed with the beauty of the rocks, needed to leave for a moment, to connect to the essence or consciousness of the Earth which received me so warmly. I began to realize that we can communicate and attune with all life forms, animate or inanimate, as we are part of a vast, unified system of consciousness, always part of the whole, never truly separate. My relationship with nature deepened tremendously.

The most recent experience of leaving my body was quite different; a deeper connection to my physical being and existence surged up from my spiritual heart, embracing me with a sweet compassion for my human experience.

I was lying asleep in my bed at home, but I kept waking up with an unusual buzzing sound in my head. I had a peculiar sensation of a vast space spinning around internally in my forehead. I was tossing and turning, wondering what these extraordinary sensations were about and, quite honestly, just wanting to fall into deep sleep. I continued to drift in and out of uneasy sleep, conscious of my body and how strangely heavy it felt. My right arm unexpectedly began to sink down through the bed. I saw what was happening, for this could not be my physical arm that continued to move down through the bed, long and light. It was my energy body moving.

"My God," I thought. "I'm coming out of my body." I began to consciously swing my energy arm back and forth until I could sense my whole body moving, or my whole energy body, as my physical self remained still. As I was doing this I was excited: I wanted to explore. In a few moments I had swung out of my physical body and was close to the edge of the bed. It was not too dark; the slight moonlight was shimmering through the light linen curtains. I began to feel a bit uneasy now, as if I should not be away from myself like this.

"What should I do now?" I thought. I continued to feel uneasy, and then I began to float upward slightly, over the bed. Wanting to look and see if I was still there, sleeping in my bed, I hovered above. I did not have a sense of my shape or form. I was definitely separate from my body, and as I looked down I saw myself. I experienced deep compassion as I looked at my own face with the moonlight softly shining on me. I had the covers tightly tucked up to my chin and my eyes were closed. I thought how beautiful this wonderful creation was. I experienced exquisite unconditional love for the young woman lying on the bed, knowing I existed beyond her, but there was a sadness to be leaving the experience of her or me behind. I experienced two parts to me then that were away from my physical body. There was the familiar mind that was thinking, "I'm out of my body, I can see myself, this is strange, and what should I do now?" But there was the other part, detached from the body, yet with strong feelings of love and compassion. My familiar mind began to panic.

"I'm not ready to leave. No, I can't leave. I want to be back in my body."

Concurrently calm and loving, knowing and detached from the mind that was panicking slightly, I continued to observe myself. My mind thought I would instantly be back in my body with having the thought of wanting to be there, but I was not. I remained above, watching.

I felt a sensation close to regret as I looked down at my body. I was leaving the Julie experience behind. Knowing I had spiritual needs to be here as Julie, I understood the sadness and regret that was present, but I began moving away from my body and the bed.

My mind was not ready to let go.

"Get back in my body, get back in my body," I pleaded. I was so still lying there on the bed.

"Oh, my God! I'm not breathing," I realized as I drifted further away from my physical being. Suddenly my physical body responded and I was aware of my chest taking in a huge breath of air; simultaneously I plunged back into my body.

Deep emotions stirred within me. The feeling of leaving my body and the deep compassion I felt was very powerful. The feeling of regret lingered, too. Had I almost died? Had I almost given up my life? For a few days afterward I was left with a slight haunting feeling, as if I had almost given up something incredibly beautiful and unique. Thinking of the experience brought tears to my eyes. It was an amazing realization of the awesome opportunity of being in a physical body, with a chance to explore the mysterious existence of being Julie.

I am consciously experiencing through a material medium made up of densely vibrating energy and space; creating, expanding, each moment new, nothing ever remaining the same. The learning was clear: be here now and appreciate this moment of life.

The awesome unconditional love I felt was forever imprinted in memory. I wish that every time I look into a mirror I can feel that for myself. How wonderful that would be. It struck me how I did not consciously love myself that way, and there was no real reason not to. How many of us, I wonder, relate to this. There are deep seeds of unworthiness, self hatred and fear, which create a sense of a separate identity, and a need to survive in this fearful world.

Chapter Eight

My Struggle and Personal Journey

Joy and Woe are woven fine
A clothing for the Soul divine
Under every grief and pine
Runs a joy with silken twine
It is right it should be so
Man is made for joy and woe
And when this we rightly know
Thro the world we safely go.
--William Blake

M Y GREATEST CHALLENGE in life manifested as an eating disorder when I was a teenager. I created my own version of hell that to a degree I lived in; it was my escape from the world and suffering, which sadly created a greater suffering within myself. Ironically, I allowed no one to see this anguish. On the surface I was living an enviable, exciting existence, hiding any pain well, even from myself initially. I did have a zest for life; I loved the outdoors, physical adventures, rock climbing, travel, a yen to learn and a warrior's disposition and determination to get out of life what I desired. But at times I was profoundly lonely. I felt a separation that I could not explain or comprehend. It took me many years to overcome the illness that haunted and ravaged my body. Yet this wounding was also a gift; I strived to overcome the pain, finding solace and connection out in nature and through meditation. I needed to understand the implications of this self destruction, the merciless hunger that harassed me, which I placated with starvation or food. I had misinterpreted it as physical hunger and food became the enemy that was trying to control me. Underneath was a starving spirit. I was emotionally and spiritually famished, unable to find a way to fulfill my spiritual yearning.

As a child I was sensitive to my outer environment, my boundaries delicately permeable. I could feel emotions and sensations that were outside of me. It was often very painful to feel what those around me felt, as well as very confusing at such a young age. The positive side of this sensitivity was the magical and delightful experience of seeing auras, colorful lights around people, trees and inanimate objects. Yet I must have learned that this was not "normal," and I began to close down my extrasensory perception, intuition and sensitivities. The eating disorder materialized as my suppressed intuitive abilities began to resurface. At a subconscious level I thought something was terribly wrong with me. I felt I needed to keep my perceptions and true self hidden. Still so young and feeling very alone, I did not have a strong container for my awareness. The spiritual rumblings were interpreted as physical hunger, and I distracted myself from my feelings with food.

I sought help in various places; ludicrously this deepened the pain and loneliness. I remember the first awful moments of acknowledging myself with an eating disorder and understanding its implications. I watched a television program on the subject, a grieving mother talking about the tragic death of her daughter through anorexia and bulimia. I was struck with terror as the realization surfaced that this could have been me. I mustered up a great deal of courage to overcome the shame and embarrassment that permeated my being, yet I knew I was on an awful track of self-destruction that was beyond my means of understanding. I shakily yet resolutely went to my family doctor. This man had been present at my birth, comforted me when I had the measles at six years old and assured me I would be fine through the all the childhood infections, coughs and colds. So terrified about the dreadful admittance of my disorder, I sat almost catatonic in his office, silently waiting to be called in. When my number was called tears filled my eyes. I so desperately needed to be free of this unbelievable nightmare that was taking over my life. Nervously I walked into his office. I sat in the old familiar oak chair bracing myself for the onslaught of tears of relief that I was sure were to come. Peering at me over his half-rimmed glasses, his familiar bushy white eyebrows a sign of comfort, the doctor waited patiently for me to speak. Tears spilled down my face, the lump in my throat barely letting the words emerge.

"I have an eating disorder," I scarcely whispered. "I really need help," I managed to unsteadily spill out. My breathing increased as my heart raced inside my chest, pounding through my ribs, anticipating his loving response. The doctor nonchalantly reached his hand over to my leg and gently gripped my thigh for a moment. Slowly taking his hand away he sat back in his chair and said rather heartlessly, "You're not that skinny."

The abysmal effects of his ignorant words sliced through me like a blunt knife. I wanted to die. My shame and embarrassment magnified. I stumbled out of his office and somehow made it home. I was appalled with myself, and the effect was to fall even deeper into the horrendous abyss.

I do not know if I had a predisposition for an eating disorder, karmic traces playing out, but likely it was the suppression of my spirituality, and my gnawing hunger for reconnection. I know it was the desolate sense of loneliness and separation that became the catalyst for the emergence of this disorder. Here I was now shutting myself off even more, terrified to let anyone know. In a way I would rather have died than to feel as misunderstood and as shameful as I did that day in the doctor's office.

It was my spiritual connection that was to eventually be my healer. Through meditation, spiritual searching and an inherent knowing that there must be some purpose in the pain, I once again began to awaken to who I was. Reaching out to God, inwardly, outwardly and through nature, the complexity and obscurity of my disorder began to smooth out, and I recognized my own inner resources for healing. I was not the eating patterns and effects — they were a product of misunderstandings in my psyche, and a calling of my soul to further itself in life.

With my sacred connection reemerging in my consciousness I began to accept myself and my unusual abilities of the sixth sense. Through reading and exploring, certain archetypal traits and patterns were revealed to me that corresponded to my life and character. Compassion and empathy brought forward an inner strength that was needed for my healing and recovery from the disorder. The depth of pain I endured at times, and the freedom of healing, inspired me to help others; thus my interest in body/mind work as a means to support others heal their emotional, physical and spiritual wounds.

In my studies of body, mind and spirit I had some incredible experiences through non-ordinary states. Many of the classes I attended as a "hands-on" practitioner were experiential and very powerful. As Ralph Waldo Emerson said, *"What lies before us and without us is but a small matter compared to what lies within us."* The journey inward has been profoundly healing for me. One of my favorite and most astounding experiences happened in a class in Hawaii.

The environment was delightful. Lush, tropical trees surrounded the rustic lodge, which had large windows overlooking the attractive, sunny gardens. The classes I was attending were fun and enriching. A wonderful mixture of experiential, tactile and perceptive work was being studied. The quiet setting and our daily sitting meditations brought an added dimension of sacredness. I was in Maui for two weeks to study visionary craniosacral work with Hugh Milne. I find Hugh's classes to be educational and profoundly thought-provoking. Hugh brought an energy of mastery to his classes, with his intrinsic knowledge and disciplined teachings.

Craniosacral work is based on a thorough knowledge of the spine and cranium anatomy. The practitioner is able to perceive and to optimize the cranial wave, the movement of the cerebrospinal fluid, by causing improved hydraulic flow patterns in the cerebrospinal fluid. This fluid baths and nourishes the brain and spinal cord. The gentle techniques used by the cranial practitioner can have profound effects on well-being as they access specific structures and psychological states. Hugh says, "Visionary craniosacral work specializes in the matters of the heart and soul." It honors both the analytical understanding of how things happen and the intuitive perception of how things really are. The work can offer profound healing and insights to the recipient. The work is done with a very light touch, usually beginning on the head, but the techniques can be used all over the body. The recipient often feels like they are floating as they merge with their inner rhythm, resulting in profound and subtle changes in the body. As emotions that have been long held in the tissues begin to release, it is possible to re-experience a past event with a detachment that makes it possible to release past trauma and to reframe an issue with ease and grace. It is not necessary to know the particulars of the trauma. Energy discharges and a new lightness of being is perceived.

In the first class we studied physiology, technique, perception and visualization. The second class focused on presence and interweaving cranial and meridian work. In traditional Chinese medicine there are twelve symmetrically paired meridians, internal pathways that constantly carry energy throughout our bodies.

It was during the second week the "Windows to the Sky" protocol was taught. This is an extremely powerful technique. Windows to the Sky refers to highly evocative locations on particular meridian points. These points are approached with great respect, and they are places of deep change and can be a catalyst into other realms.

I was to be the receiving model as Maureen, one of the teachers, demonstrated to the class. I lay down on the table and began to relax. The students eagerly gathered around with notebooks and pens as the teacher began her demonstration. I had no idea what was about to occur; only expecting to get a good sense of the protocol by receiving it.

It seems appropriate to comment on the previous day's encounters, as the synchronistic events have some significance to the story.

It was our day off in between the classes. A small group of us had gone to the beach to enjoy Maui's golden sand and warm, inviting ocean. To our dismay a huge storm cloud appeared above us and began to pour warm raindrops heavily down on us. We sought shelter under a large tree, and waiting for the rain to stop, we snuggled close together and began to chat. We were talking about our negative and positive aspects, a continued discussion from what had emerged in class, and how the negative, the shadow part of ourselves, comes through in behavior patterns we would rather not be acting out. A deep and intimate conversation began as we huddled closely together trying to keep warm; the great tree was protecting us with its strong leafy branches from the unyielding rain. I talked about an energy I was aware of — a deep aspect of my darker side that I felt needed to be met; the same energy that was connected to my disordered eating, the traces of which I was still aware of and extremely careful about.

"You've got to get to know your dark side to release and transform it," one of the girls offered.

"I know that mentally," I responded, "But it's actually doing it, the darker parts of our psyche are not necessarily inviting. I know this is energy and it needs to be released, or at the very least acknowledged so it doesn't hold power over me. I suppose I can tap into this energy and confront it through intention, but it feels really dark and ugly, kind of frightening to face by myself."

"Don't worry Julie, there's always light after the dark." We all laughed a bit, wanting to lighten up.

With that the storm clouds began to break up and the hot sun shone its warm and bright rays down on us again. We ran for the ocean splashing and jumping, enjoying the delights of the day like children, forgetting everything we had talked about. A little while later, exhausted with play, we lay drying ourselves on the sand, and a couple came over with their didgeridoo, an Australian Aborigine instrument.

"Would you like to be played on?" The exotic-looking girl asked, brown eyes twinkling and smiling as I looked up to her.

"What do you mean?" I asked curiously.

"If you don't mind I'll show you."

I relaxed with the warm sand below me, the radiant sun shining above me. The beautiful girl began to blow into the long didgeridoo. She moved it slowly a few inches above my body in small circles. I immediately felt a tingling sensation as the vibration danced merrily in my energy field.

"It can help to bring balance into your life," she said.

She played on the other girls and then it was time to for us to leave — we had class early the next morning and we wanted to get a good night's sleep.

I had forgotten all about the previous day's adventure as I lay quietly on the table that next day. I began to take advantage of being able to feel and hear the protocol as Maureen gently began to move through the points on my upper body and explain what they were.

Tuned into my body, I became aware of a strange sensation, a feeling that a dense liquid was running down through me from the crown of my head, bringing heightened sensitivity to my whole being. My body began to feel extremely heavy.

"How are you feeling, Julie?" Maureen asked.

"I am more in my body than ever before, like every piece of my spirit is squeezing itself down through me. It's quite peculiar," I answered trying to articulate the impressions.

As the sensation hit the very end of my toes, a thunder bolt of energy struck me. I, or this new energy inside me, was thrown backward, as if it were being pushed violently out of my body, but my body went, too. I went head first off the end of the table. Maureen and the observers rushed to hold me and help me as I slipped onto the floor. No one knew quite what was happening, yet everyone was experienced with the potential of quick movements and altered states in this work, so I was quite safe.

I was catapulted into the depths of darkness — pitch black, ancient, isolated, secluded from any source of light. A primal scream suddenly came shuddering through my body; my fist went to my mouth as I tried to reach something deep inside me, as if trying to drag the convoluted crying out. The scream was muffled but so powerful I thought it would tear my body apart.

Archaic fear pierced my being. More than a feeling, a real

pulsating existence had emerged, a vast power so overwhelming and beyond me it had cast me aside as it lived through me. I experienced it as an organism terrified of the light which emanated from the people around me. No longer in control of my body or my senses, I was barely aware. The students tried to calm me. I, or I as it, became outraged; their radiance was painful. I crawled backward on the floor, scurrying away from them, scraping my chin and fists. Deep guttural screams continued to come from my belly, reverberating around the room. My fists burnt on the carpet as I kept pushing myself back, trying to escape them, the echoes of my own scream trying to wake me from this nightmare, yet I seemed far away. Part of me left my body and for a moment I was floating above the scene. I saw my body crouched and backing up like a strange, terrified creature. I saw Hugh walking around the edge of the room, carefully watching, and Maureen reaching out her hand to me. Then I was instantly back in my body.

I felt an awesome isolation which was all-consuming, and I experienced almost complete dissolution of awareness of myself. I had become identified with the consciousness of this unimaginable terror, but a fraction of myself or true mind, was watching, calm and accepting, somewhere seemingly far away, distant yet present.

With one final, primeval scream I fell flat to the ground, exhausted. Lying on the carpet, my heart and head pounded rapidly as my blood rushed frantically around inside me. I became motionless, immense nothingness like a desolate void surrounded me. Quiet darkness appeared, and eventually calmness entered my being and a light began to filter into my inner vision.

In the stillness I recognized that love was pouring into my weary body. I could feel it in my heart like sweet honey nourishing my soul. Experiencing exquisite love, there was only love now and I was loved. I opened my eyes, no longer scared or alone and through the tears I saw a numinous image of the Virgin Mary — a beautiful, unexpected sight. I could see her compassionate, loving eyes, her face shrouded in a soft blue veil, and luminous light glowing about her as she looked lovingly into my eyes. She was holding me gently in her arms. Having broken out of the encapsulation and isolation of separation, my body senses returned. My spatial boundaries transformed; I was a delicate soft baby. I could feel my smallness, innocence, and helplessness, and I had total trust in the arms that cradled me.

Another curious transformation began as I became Mary, the mother, holding the baby. I was unconditional love, understanding, knowing and nurturance. Every cell in my body began another exhilarating transformation as I became mother and baby, a trillion awesome simultaneous experiences of absolute loving. Exuberant bliss filling me, it was all incredible. I experienced the mother and the baby simultaneously, miraculously experiencing both concurrently. The melding was so utterly complete. I had lost the identity of my own body — my mind shattered at the enormity of the experience, unable to make any sense of how real this was. The feeling multiplied over and over, ecstasy rolled through me as love unfolded blissfully, over and over again, never ending, infinite love. I surrendered into the bliss, letting go to the beauty and depth of this extraordinary state of being.

As I returned to an ordinary state, I found myself surrounded by my fellow students and friends. Having witnessed a bizarre incident, they patiently waited until I came back allowing me to complete the process. As my body and mind returned to familiar consciousness, my girlfriend Shannon took my head in her lap, and stroked my head until I was fully present. Hours had passed, class was well over and Shannon and I decided to walk outside into the emerging evening. We leisurely strolled up the small grassy hill overlooking the luscious Hawaiian landscape. The night began to settle in, and darkness fell, the unfaltering stars appeared, twinkling lovingly overhead.

"What a miracle it is to be alive," I thought enthusiastically. "What a beautiful mystery."

I allowed the days events to integrate without thinking too much about it. My mind was very perplexed at experiencing transcendence of my physical boundaries, in such a dramatic and dynamic manner. The darkness and terror had been so consuming and real. It felt like it had been beyond me, but I hold a small piece of it within me. I had journeyed into the wholeness of it, experiencing the illusion of the separation from God from such a deep perspective. The enormity of experiencing Mother and Child in one experiential continuum was awesome and humbling. I knew an intrinsically arcane journey had transpired. I felt lighter as time went by; something important had been released from my psyche. The power and reason of my past eating disorder seemed to make more sense to me, and another level of healing had taken place. The internal hunger I had carried for a deeper connection to Spirit had resulted in the cavernous separation I felt, or was it the other way around? I had sought refuge in behavior that exiled me from the world of Spirit at times, and left me with an insatiable hunger. I still had wounds deep inside that occasionally haunted me. The Great Mother archetype had surfaced, penetrating the deepest levels of existence of darkness, bringing into conscious the unconscious for healing. I realized how deeply in my psyche the feeling of separation was, and ultimately embedded within the cosmos, in each of us. I found greater clarity of the deep hunger for connection that had haunted me through life, and was able to release much of it through this experience.

Chapter Nine

Is Who
You See
Who You Are?

If the doors of perception were cleansed, everything would
appear to manifest as it is, infinite.

–William Blake

THE WEEK AFTER THE REMARKABLE event of the "Windows to the Sky" protocol, another strange encounter came about. At the end of the week following the class, I had two days to explore the island. The first day I decided to hike down the fantastic 10,000 foot Healekala volcano, absorbing myself in the beautiful colors of the rock. Reds, yellows, gold and black were warm and intriguing, tracing the courses of recent and ancient lava flows. The inspiring wilderness and unusual landscape thrilled me as I walked down and back up to watch the sunset. It was a perfectly spiritual and grounding day after such an emotionally charged week.

The following day two of the students had asked me to join them back at the lodge where they were going to meet with an oracle, Ariel.

To be honest, I was not quite sure what an oracle was. Maureen and Kelly explained to me that an oracle was one who gave answers. They both knew of Ariel and had heard astonishing and exciting information about her from people they knew and trusted. I had free time and it sounded quite intriguing.

Ariel was to meet us at the lodge. Maureen and Kelly were obviously excited at the prospect of meeting with Ariel. I felt neutral as the last two weeks had been full enough, and I had no expectations. I also did not have any questions that had come forward for me to ask. I was just filling time really and feeding my curiosity about an oracle.

I walked into the small, plain bedroom where Ariel was waiting. She was sitting comfortably on the bed. I noticed her shoulder-length blond hair flowing softly around her gentle features. I immediately felt at ease, and my actions surprised me. I walked right over to the bed and sat beside her, like it was the most natural thing to do, and I smiled. She returned a knowing smile to me. This seemed a little out of the ordinary for me, not choosing to sit on a chair. I was so comfortable, it did not occur to me I may have been rude or over-presumptuous to park on the bed beside her so easily. She seemed unaffected by my sitting next to her. Maureen and Kelly sat on chairs beside the bed. She began talking to Maureen first.

It was a powerful dialogue; Ariel's words evoked deep emotions from Maureen. I was surprised though by how little she actually said, it was more her presence and empathic demeanor. She did not actually tell Maureen anything new, but touched her by her incredible knowing and guidance. The same occurred with Kelly. I thought the whole thing was quite profound and gentle, and I was pleased to be there witnessing it. When Ariel turned to me I had no idea what was about to unfold.

She looked deeply into my eyes, and began by telling me things about my childhood. How could she know these intimate details of my child nature? She knew of my intuitiveness, my innermost feelings and my relationship to God. I was truly mystified. This was not how I had experienced her talking to my friends. She explained it was very unusual for her to tell anyone anything, yet this was a special circumstance. She recognized me! Her precious, loving presence eased me, as what followed was quite surprising. As she talked I watched her features softly change — her face grew thinner and younger as her skin smoothed out and a luminous glow surrounded her. She looked so beautiful and soft. I continuously looked into her blue eyes. Her gaze never left mine, and she continued to talk softly to me. I was aware of Maureen and Kelly crying gently, captivated and moved by the unfolding episode. I felt caught in an enchanting spell and I did not want to move my eyes from hers. As I watched, her eyes became totally and fantastically white; the peculiar sight was mystically entrancing. Her voice now resonated deeply inside me, and I was mesmerized.

Her tale continued. "You are not of this earth," she said assuredly, "but from a distant planet. Your journey here is to just be. Your vibratory rate is a frequency that will affect those around you, raising consciousness to a higher level." She smiled lovingly. "Don't worry, you will attract others like you, you won't be alone."

Her eyes changed again, this time green and lizard-like. Time seemed to freeze as I sat in the iridescent glow emanating from her. Eternal moments slipped by before she transformed back into her original face. "Another planet," I thought. "Well that is interesting. It would probably make a lot of sense to Sam, since he had suggested that on numerous occasions," I laughed to myself.

Our time with Ariel came to an end; we all took deep breaths, trying to assimilate what we experienced, and began to say our goodbyes.

I felt quite sad at her leaving, as there was a loving motherly quality that I wanted to stay close to. Unsure how I felt about what she said, I was taking it all very lightly. I had tremendously enjoyed her company and the rich experience. Apart from that, the shape-shifting was really incredible to witness. I asked Maureen about it, and she too had experienced similar images as she looked into Ariel's eyes. We did not quite know what to make of it. I have witnessed this phenomenon frequently though, since. To look into a person's face and see its features transform is quite astonishing. One of the most vivid experiences of this kind came when Sam and I were out in the desert one day hiking with our friend Jimmy.

We had spent a great day walking and enjoying the rocks and unusual flora out in Joshua Tree in Southern California. Before sunset, we chose a good vantage point so we could comfortably watch the day come to a close as the sun elegantly dropped down into the distant horizon.

Jimmy stood a few feet in front of me, and Sam sat at my side. Outrageous, beautiful colors began to electrify the sky, illuminating the tranquil desert. This time of day is always magical, often described as the time between the worlds, where the numinous reveals itself. I looked at Jimmy and to my greatest surprise, his whole being began to distinctively change shape, at least six different times. One after another a new mesmerizing figure appeared before me with different attire, and all radiating a unique vibration that sizzled through me vicariously. I had never seen this shape-shifting so vivid and dramatic. My body shivered and tingled with each sensational transformation. There was the tall image of a man shrouded in white animal skins, exuding power. Another was a dark figure, tall and skinny, whose dark energy and overwhelming gaze evoked a discomforting stir of my energy. My eyes filled with tears as the exhilarating alchemy continued.

"How do you do that Jimmy?" I asked in awe. His familiar face and eyes looked at me, laughing, and I was sure he knew what was happening. I was crying and laughing now because of the extraordinariness and clarity of the event. I realized he was a bit perplexed at my reaction though. "You know what I'm seeing, right?"

He did not, and when I told him what I saw, he just shook his head in wonder. He had been focusing on his kundalini energy, the potent life force energy that lies coiled up in the sacrum, at the bottom of the spine. He could sense its gentle shift through his body as it moved upward through his spine. He did not realize the effect it was having. Jimmy is a healer and a musician who also practices shamanic journeying in this lifetime. Was I witnessing the images of his past or simultaneous lives as a Shaman, a Seer and Sorcerer?

Another interesting time I witnessed shape-shifting was at a seminar on breathwork given by a lecturer from Harvard who had an avid interest in Shamanism. As we sat in the opening circle I looked at the teacher and his face changed drastically. If I looked at others next to him nothing occurred, yet each time I looked at him this shape-shifting took place. During the workshop we discussed Shamanism and I felt it would be appropriate to ask him if he knew what I was seeing. He did not, and he had no answers for me. He said one other time someone had experienced the same thing with him, only he had watched her shift also. They apparently recognized each other from previous lives together. He did not see me change, nor did we recognize one another.

I am sometimes able to change my vibratory rate, and I see my own face transform in the mirror. This can be quite exhilarating. I have seen faces of male and female, all uniquely mesmerizing and slightly familiar to me. To explain what this is like for those who have not experienced it, it would be similar to looking at a holographic picture, when it is turned slightly, the image changes, revealing a new picture. Now imagine each time the image changes you feel a light shiver run through your body as the eyes look directly at you, expressionless, but very much alive. In a holographic universe, location, time and space exist in one continuum. Am I tuning into frequencies that decipher the past, or indeed the future, revealing images of what has been, what is to come, or what is now? Who is to say that I am seeing lives of our past, for time is of our making. Maybe when I die my next birth will be in the thirteenth century. And of course there is the interesting thought that beyond our experience of the space/time continuum, all of our lives are happening simultaneously. There is not time or space here to go into the theories and concepts of a holographic universe: location ceases to exist, all points in space are equal, nothing is separate from anything else and all of us are part of a whole. Therefore I will simply quote William Blake's well-known and beautiful poem, where he captures so eloquently the interconnectedness of the universe:

> *To see a world in a grain of sand*
> *And heaven in a wild flower,*
> *Hold infinity in the palm of your hand*
> *And eternity in an hour.*

Chapter Ten

Beyond the Personal

Lord, help me...
Because my boat is so small,
And your sea so immense.
–French medieval prayer

I WOKE WITH A START; MY BODY was vibrating intensely as an internal energy coursed through my veins. I looked at the clock. It was only 5 AM — too early to be getting up, but I was wide awake. My night had been full of vivid and exciting adventures; I had been flying, and as I came back to my sleeping self with tremendous speed, the sensation of a quick entry back into my body woke me up. I felt unusually alert and energized for such an early hour, and wide awake. I realized I was not going back to sleep, and though I rarely get up at this early hour, it seemed the best thing to do. I decided to practice some yoga. After an hour of practicing asanas my body was still feeling overloaded with vibrating energy, so I decided to go outside for a run. The room felt stifling and the thought of the cool morning air filling my lungs was enticing. Outside the air was refreshing, and the day vibrant. With the birds singing sweetly, and the sky a clear, turquoise blue I felt really wonderful as I ran through the quiet, tree-lined streets of Santa Monica.

This particular weekend I was in school studying for an MA in spiritual psychology. Class usually finished quite late, and rather than driving the long way home at 10 PM I would spend the evenings at a nearby hotel.

After my run I showered, jovially singing to myself, ate breakfast, then left for class. I arrived at school that morning at ten o'clock still feeling great. The vibration that had filled my body so early had lessened, leaving me feeling very light and high-spirited. I did not give it much thought other than that it was the residual sensation of being out of my body, which can be quite wonderful.

Class began with a short prayer and a five minute silent peace meditation. I thought of my mum, family and friends, and my thoughts just continued to expand outward. I did not know where to stop, until I was sending love to all beings. My hands were out on my lap, and into my imagination came the appearance of our planet. I visualized holding the planet in my palms, embracing it with loving, healing energy. I could feel enormous, heartfelt gratitude and love as I sat for the five minutes, deeply immersed in the expansive meditation, feeling loving energy fill me and spill down my arms into the imaginary planet. When the meditation came to a close, I was feeling very centered and calm. Our class went on as usual until my reality was shattered that afternoon with a spontaneous and overwhelming event that left me spellbound and rapt with possibilities.

I experienced a dynamic movement of kundalini energy. The experience took me, my individual experience as a being, to a mergence with a planetary consciousness. To understand this better, one could look at the human body as a symbolic representation of something much greater, the whole, so each of us is, in a way, a reflection of the entire universe. If we look at the world for a moment as a stage, then each of us, as actors, hold the drama of the planet within us. Each one of us holds the potential to heal not only our own wounds in the role we play, but the planetary consciousness that our particular role or energy is connected to. Each one of us is a spark of the unified field of cosmic consciousness. We are a microcosm of the macrocosm — expanding, contracting and creating on our way back to the whole, which we are actually never separate from. This understanding came to me after the experience, and because it was more than a cognitive experience, but an experience on many levels, it resonates at a very deep level of truth within me. The dynamic energy ignited certain energy centers, or chakras, within my subtle body that opened me up to an amazing array of consciousnesses. My experience was spontaneous, and rising within me came a mosaic matrix of realities.

There were over two hundred of us, gathered to watch a three-minute video segment with an intense emotional content. A group of individuals were discussing the trauma of having a family member murdered, the anger and grief the family members suffered, and then the healing power of forgiveness that came later. I remember only the first few seconds or so, for I was overcome with a peculiar energy that took me out of ordinary consciousness.

My physical boundaries dissolved, and I was given entry into supersensory realms. I remember it happening in slow motion. My head turned away from the screen, a thick energy encased my being, and I felt as if I were flying back through time. The depth of the darkness around me felt incredible; it was dense and heavy, and I immediately lost sense of my body. The students were sitting in groups of three, and as the video finished, each group moved into their discussion. As my partners turned to face me, they saw me sitting strangely still, with eyes closed, but eyelids fluttering. They gave me a couple of minutes to maybe assimilate the information, or process the emotion from the video, but after a short while, realized something was amiss. They called my name yet I did not respond; one of the girls went to get help from one of our teachers.

They could not have known what was happening, and I was not able to tell — so deep in an altered state that I was unable to pull myself free. I felt a part of myself as vast awareness, detached but knowing something important was occurring. Witnessing the whole thing, I hypnotically rode the experience each moment. It was not particularly easy from the perspective of my ordinary mind, so surrendering to the experience was the best I could do; but I am not really sure I even had a choice, the force was so powerful.

I experienced a series of images simultaneously, strangely and horrifyingly real. It was unimaginable how they could all be happening at once, but in an instant I saw and experienced so much. I was a part of every scene, yet still strangely removed, witnessing without emotion as planes of consciousness flowered before me, revealing what was usually imperceptible. Terrifying, raging fires, blood stained swords and thousands of agonizing faces swirled around me; I was amidst unimaginable scenes of torture, crucifixion, unjust death, pain and anguish.

I then began to feel my own body then being pulled into the reality before me. A thick ugly rope tightened around my own neck and my wrists were tightly bound. Hungry flames from a raging fire leapt about me and licked at my suffering body. Tormented voices screamed out in pain all about me, and I was all of them; death was being screamed for, hatred and hysteria was rampaging through the crowds around me.

"I love you, I love you," I whispered, hearing my own voice here. Yet I was calling out in some other time, some other place. I was calm, even though now I felt part of the horrific scenes. Compassion and love soared through me, and my heart felt like it was a balloon filling up with love and compassion until it exploded outward, embracing all those dying around me as well as to those who were responsible for the killing.

"I am not afraid, I am not angry, I forgive you." I felt these words like a loving river spill through the images, releasing the terror and the pain of wherever I was.

Then I was being pulled back into present time, into the classroom. I heard the teacher calling my name. I opened my eyes; the people around me seemed so distant. I felt caught between two worlds. I knew it was important to let them know I was okay. I drank the water they gave me. Looking into their eyes, and nodding my head at their questions, "Yes I'm okay, yes I'm here." I assured them, needing to seem somewhat rational, yet feeling anything but, I knew the experience was occurring in transrational realm.

I tried desperately to hold on to this reality, afraid I might have been seen as having a psychotic episode, or unable to contain my emotions at an "acceptable level." It was frightening to me to be so vulnerable in the proximity of so many people, yet I had little time for these thoughts and feelings. To look back, I am surprised to see how strong the ego/mind is, even amidst the most incredible transcending experience. I was experiencing the duality within me — "little me" versus the "I am." And each time I was in present time/awareness, I was afraid of the judgments, and the isolation the awesome experience could bring. I remembered from sometime long ago the secrecy needed to protect the holiness of mystery.

Just trying to appear somewhat present was taking up all my energy. I tried to talk but my hands began to ache and burn as I could still feel the tight ropes around them. The strange events began to bleed through from one reality to the other.

I felt the rope gone from my wrists, but the pain became quite intense, as if all life force had been cut off from them and was now unmercifully pouring back in. They felt swollen to three times their normal size. I tried to shake the feeling free of them and then watched as they moved slowly, distorting and twisting beyond my control, strange ritualistic gestures, releasing the energy in their own way.

I tried to talk for a while, seeing if I could be coherent, but I was still deeply in the experience. I was holding both levels of consciousness at once for a while, but it was useless. A rope was bound around my throat, it twisted my neck and I was hung a thousand times over. I went again into a deep trance.

The next sequences of events elude me a little, but I remember a wave of laughter swept unmercifully through me. I laughed hysterically, crazily, yet desperately trying to laugh silently so not to disturb people around me – my little mind again afraid of its annihilation by others. My senses had acutely intensified. All images were gone now, but my body was reacting to the internal complexities that had begun. As soon as I could contain the laughter, which was incredibly difficult to do, I was able to leave my seat. With the teacher walking beside me, I was so sensitive to everything around me during those moments that if she held my arm, as she wanted to do, I felt like I would have exploded with sensory overload. I also wanted as little attention drawn to me as possible. I felt aware of everyone's feelings, emotions and thoughts in the room, moments of amazing psychic ability, which would have been too much to bear if their thoughts were directed toward me in concern.

Sitting in a chair in the back of the room, the kundalini energy rose along my Sushumna Channel, the inner channel of the astral spine. Different states of consciousness were experienced and strange inner lights were now flashing through my body. A large vibrant eye appeared in the vast space of my inner vision, and my heart was beating so sporadically I thought it would surely explode. I was extremely aware of the huge energy current as it surged through me, I was not concerned with my health; I was in awe of what was happening.

Still in an extremely altered state, energy began coursing through my whole body, causing my legs to shake. Explosions of color were going off inside me. Accompanying the swelling feeling in my solar plexus was a visual experience of color, and I was aware of strange dimensions within me — universes and galaxies forming with tremendous explosions right inside of me. The brilliance of letting go of identification with an embodied self was evident, as I participated intimately and blissfully in creation. The essential nature of the phenomenal creation of the universe was transcendental and numinous. The afterglow of the beautiful revelations vibrated ecstatically for a long while afterward.

"All is within us," I recall thinking. All the while the teacher sat lovingly with me, talking to me, keeping eye contact so I would not leave my present awareness. I still could not explain coherently what was happening. I knew what was taking place, but it felt difficult to relate this experience at the time. I just wanted to let go, to let my body shake violently to release the incredible force within me. I could feel it spinning upward inside me, and I wanted to spin around and around with it, yet I stayed still, keeping eye contact, and listening to the teacher. My head was so full of energy I literally had to pull my hair upward creating space, so as to release the force. I knew it was important not to contain this vast energy within me. The chakras are gateways to release and transform energy, so the reservoirs can flow freely, keeping internal balance. This applies not just to the energies of this magnitude, but to energy of emotions like fear, upset and anger, so we do not contain them and create blockages within our subtle bodies.

As the energy began to subside an hour or so later, I went to the bathroom. The people I passed seemed strange, their faces changing as I looked at them, revealing a multitude of images. I wanted to wash my hands, yet water became vulgar. I was repulsed by its magnetic nature and so I just let this be, nothing now being too unusual.

Over two hours later I was back to a normal enough state to where no one would know that I had experienced anything unusual. I could function normally while still in deep communion with my transcendental Self. Class finished early that night, so at nine o'clock I went for a slow walk around the neighborhood. My heart began to beat rapidly again, so I began to breathe deeply, consciously and calmly before going back to the hotel.

I called Sam, and we talked for an hour. He promised to keep the phone by the bed, and got me to promise if anything else happened, especially with energy surges in my heart, to call him. I could only sleep for a few hours that night, my body trembling slightly as the energy continued to sweep through me. Irregular beats in my heart kept me conscious as the powerful energy revitalized me; all the while I was feeling a deep love and compassion for all of humanity.

I always like to write and record my dreams after a powerful experience, as I find there is usually some learning contained in it for me. I had a beautiful dream when I did sleep that night:

> *I am on an island, attending school, yet I am the only one there apart from a strikingly gorgeous, large white owl and her baby. I am learning about sight, magic and the powerful forces of energy.*

I had just recently dreamt of owl, and wrote:

> *I see a huge white owl sitting in a tree. I climb the tree*
> *to reach the owl and I am tiny in comparison to the*
> *awesome bird. I safely reach it and snuggle into the soft*
> *white feathers. It takes flight and we fly to a medieval*
> *castle, where it lands on the high fortress wall and we face*
> *the rising sun, watching with great reverence the dawning*
> *of a new day.*
>
> *Owls have an aura of mystery, birds of the night. The*
> *night symbolizes the darkness within us, yet these myste-*
> *rious birds can see in the darkest of nights. Owl can teach*
> *us the secrets of the dark; it is the bird of magic, prophecy*
> *and wisdom.*

From a cosmic view point, I knew I had somehow melded with some planetary consciousness as powerful energy moved through me. The love and compassion that exploded within me was part of a healing force. It was purely spiritual, beyond the personal, and to this day I remain humbled at the whole event, which continues to reveal itself.

Through the following three weeks, I would feel this new energy move through me, especially around my sacrum area. Occasionally I would move into spontaneous laughter, and experience a great feeling of joy and love. The memories of the cosmic explosions, magnificent manifestations of universes, continued to stretch the horizon of my mind. I kept myself very grounded by eating more food and doing more vigorous exercises. I do not have a teacher or guide present to help me in daily life with these happenings, so I ceased my yoga and meditation practice for a short while, until I felt that I was no longer suscep-tible to another extreme rising. I ran in the canyon most days, feeling like I was dispersing the excess energy from inside me, keeping connected to the earth. I did not have another strong movement of energy until New Years Eve, three weeks later.

I was visiting friends in Ojai. Sam and I planned to receive a Shiatsu session from our friend Jimmy, before we spent the rest of the day with him and his wife, to celebrate the coming New Year. Throughout my session I was aware of the movement of energy through the meridians, channels inside the body that Jimmy was working on to help my internal energy move freely. Once the session was over I moved deeply into an altered state. I sat on the couch in the office, Jimmy sitting with me, observing the changes within me. He noted how deeply I had gone in the session, and so we just sat waiting until I was back in an ordinary state, but it did not happen for a while.

I could sense a great feeling bubble up within me and giggles began to escape me. Before long I was falling about with uncontrollable laughter. Everything in life just seemed so funny and beautiful. I was so glad I knew Jimmy and he was able to sit with me for awhile until the energy settled down. He sat observing with a gentle smile, and then covered me with a blanket. I lay still, with just small spurts of laughter breaking through the silence. My body naturally began to move into yoga postures, and here I stayed until I felt I could get up a short while later. I could feel the energy inside me contracting and expanding; as it contracted, my muscles tensed up, and as I expanded I would move into laughter and joy, or my body would again spontaneously take up a yoga posture for a while. The specific postures freed and grounded the energy. Jimmy had also experienced a kundalini awakening, and I was grateful for his presence and words of wisdom as he graciously allowed me to move through the experience with freedom, so I did not feel inhibition or embarrassment. When I felt the energy moving up through me in a spinning motion, I actually felt able to move with it. I slowly spun around on my hands and knees, and then my body took up another posture. I felt freedom and a wonderful sense of alignment as the experience unfolded. I have remained still and detached from these experiences when they happen in meditation; sometimes the stillness takes me to another level, yet sometimes it is fruitless and the movement becomes paramount.

After an hour or so Sam and I returned to our hotel where I took a hot bath, and once again returned to my "normal" self.

Knowing the experiences were emergence of kundalini energy allowed me to honor them and myself. The bioelectric energy of kundalini is also known as Shakti. Shakti is said to lie dormant, taking the shape of a great white serpent, coiling around the sacrum three and a half times, seen as the ephemeral, kinetic feminine aspect of the twin principles of the Godhead. She lies asleep, and when manifested, is the kundalini Shakti. The changeless, static aspect of consciousness is Shiva, also lying dormant, residing at the crown chakra at the top of the head. Together Shiva and Shakti form a duality in which Shiva is the power holder and Shakti the power itself. Shiva and Shakti do lie within the realms of the human body; when kundalini is awakened, she will rise, and if joined with Shiva, nothing stands in the way of oneself merging with cosmic consciousness. Anyone of us, though, can have spontaneous surges of kundalini energy to various energy centers, bringing forth an expansion of awareness and higher levels of consciousness.

As each major energy center or chakra, of which we have seven, is ignited by the powerful source, we can move into amazing bliss, or our internal demons and the dark realms of our psyche, can surface. It can be a stormy ride, accompanied by periods of ecstasy, depression and confusion. How often has a kundalini awakening been diagnosed as insanity, or depression, or another incorrect label because of the ignorance of the West, or its denial at the possibility of such a phenomenon? This was my initial fear as the energy coursed through me in school, though I knew the reality of what was happening to me.

Through experiences like the above, I am always left with a deep humility. They are unfathomably profound and I usually feel no desire to talk about them, yet a yearning from my heart to express, kept pushing me forward in writing this book. What also held me back in the past was a deep-rooted fear that I could not justify mentally; but the bottom line felt like I would be annihilated if I revealed my truth — death would be imminent. As irrational as this belief was, it felt real; but I eventually transcended this fear.

Insightful enough to know something was brewing internally, I left, seeking sanctuary in a retreat center in Arizona. There, I experienced a tremendous period of ecstatic energy emergences that took me to new levels of consciousness.

One morning I was walking around the quiet desert garden, observing a deep sadness within me, not knowing what it was about. I was feeling lonely and separate without any particular reason. I decided to receive an acupuncture session that afternoon to see if the energy could be released. About five minutes into the session I began to cry. A lot of emotion began to move through me until my heart felt as if it would break, and then my inner vision opened up to reveal past lives of myself being killed. The most vivid scenes were of being burned in a fire until all that remained were charred flesh and bones. Black, burnt remnants of a physical existence, mercilessly destroyed by those that feared its Soul's truth. I watched — I was the body in the flames, and the flames themselves; I was the crying despair and I was the horror of injustice. The chamber of my vision seized powerful endurance as I mingled with the river of time gone by. Waves of energy moved through and off me as I observed and experienced, releasing memory, and once the images faded I felt a great sense of peace, calm and internal strength. I released the storage of energy that kept me fearful of speaking my truth. It appeared that I had been killed for speaking my truth before and the energy of fear was still with me in this lifetime. I no longer feel as if I have to apologize for what I see, what I know, and what I experience. It is my truth, and I think to share stories with one another is a wonderful way to communicate — to reach a deeper understanding of who we are. How we receive the story is, of course, our individual choice.

Chapter Eleven

Heartbreak
and *Soul Pain*

A human being is part of the whole called by us universe, a part limited in time and space. He experiences himself, his thoughts and feelings as something separate from the rest, a kind of optical delusion of his consciousness. This delusion is a kind of prison for us, restricting us to our personal desires and to affection for a few persons nearest to us. Our task must be to free ourselves from this prison by widening our circle of compassion to embrace all living creatures and the whole of nature in its beauty.
–Albert Einstein

THERE HAVE BEEN A FEW TIMES in my life when I feel I have tuned into the soul of the planet. By this I mean a huge feeling that is transpersonal, beyond my individual self. This is not so unusual; many people are sensitive to their environment and to the further reaches of the mind. For example, after a major disaster, earthquake or flood, often just before I hear about it on the news, the feelings from beyond rise from deep within me, as a profound part of the larger being of who I am. Intuition is a birthright many of us are just beginning to tune into. It is our gift, our intimate connection. This of course makes sense when we view ourselves as a part of the whole, a flame of an eternal fire or a drop of the infinite ocean. We all encounter such realizations at some level, and are affected by it, yet do not always realize our ability to contribute to the healing. Of course many of us do. The prayers and loving thoughts that are sent to victims of disasters, the contributions and donations and the feelings that are invoked in us are all part of the necessary experience to heal ourselves and the planet. I remember the airplane crash in Lockerbie, Scotland many years ago — the eerie knowing that an awful event had occurred and then the sadness that I carried when my precognition was confirmed. I could not imagine what it must have been like for the community, but the effects could be felt all over the world.

The energy often runs through the heart — the heart chakra known as the seat of Brahma. In the Hindu tradition Lord Brahma is traditionally known as the creator of the universe. The heart is also known as the bridge between the worlds, the gateway to the astral level. Through the astral level we can feel the environment, sense the moods and feelings of others, or know the atmosphere of a room before or when we enter it. Most of have been consciously aware of that experience at some time in our life. I was in Africa, September 2001 — a month that we will all remember for the tragic events that happened in America, which rippled around the world. I experienced such a heartfelt emotion of unfathomable sadness it overwhelmed me, yet I had no idea what was happening.

The disaster began on the eve of September the eleventh, Kenya time, so it was the morning of the eleventh in New York. I could not sleep and my heart was pounding erratically. I would have been more worried had I not just recently had a complete physical exam and knew everything was in great shape. So this night, with my heart pounding and intense energy sweeping through it, I got up out of my bed. Unsure what it was about, I went to the bathroom and sat on the edge of the tub to think. Sam was sleeping; I did not want to wake him as we were planning our ascent up Kilimanjaro the next day. I was hoping I would feel fine in a short while. The prospect of hiking up any significant elevation seemed unlikely though at this time. My thoughts retraced my day; nothing I ate or drank could have been causing this. I was looking forward to the climb, and we were not yet at any elevation. I had traveled around the world climbing and hiking, yet my heart was aching and acting as if I was having a massive anxiety attack, which I assumed would feel somewhat similar. I became more concerned. Being far from any medical facility, the thought of being ill in Africa was not appealing to me at all.

Sam woke up and came to see where I was. I told him how awful I was feeling, and also how very sad, as if my heart was breaking. We talked for a while, wondering what was going on; why such a deep sadness and anxiety that it was making me cry. There really seemed nothing we could do except try to sleep. Deep in my heart I knew something terrible was taking place — a dismaying expression of grief of the collective human soul, chilling as it resonated through me in the warm Kenya night. At last I did fall asleep, but my night was filled with disturbing dreams. I remember hearing distressing calls from children crying out for daddy, and the chilling cries for help echoed around the night. I was still feeling very sad when I woke up in the morning, but we decided to go on with our journey as my heartbeat seemed to have returned to normal, and we knew we could turn back if anything happened. I love Africa. I was so looking forward to camping and climbing Mount Kilimanjaro that I may have gone on until my heart gave out. Being in nature is the epitome of who I am. When the awesome land got into my blood, I became so attuned with the environment. I felt so vibrantly alive, close to God, and a sense of holy unity, that I could not imagine turning back. The peace of the land, with such affection, embraced me, and the thoughts of disaster slowly faded.

As I sat on the mountain, I blended with the flawlessness of nature. Silence was all around, but for the occasional calls of animals in the distant. Paradise. As we hiked upward, the thrill of seeing herds of elephants, tracks of big cats hunting on the lonely mountainside and the awesome stretch of blazing land below enthralled me. We walked through sweet ancient jungles, the monkeys peering wildly at us through the dense and beautiful trees. Native children sat playing in the earth, solitary moments of connection as our eyes met briefly and I wonder what, if any, impact these strange travelers may have had on them. I was taken into wonder of who they were, who they would become and the scarcity of their lives, those who still live with the land. For awhile the sadness was forgotten as I concentrated on the journey. Soon we were high enough where there were no animals, no people — unscathed, glorious naked land, so breathtaking the entire world should have it touch their senses. This is our planet, and it bothers me that so few experience its natural wonder. The grand peak with its awesome snow cap and magnificent glacier towering above us at almost twenty thousand feet, beckoned to our adventurous souls. Below, the great land of Kenya, with its myriad of wildlife and native peoples, shimmered perfectly under the hot African sun. The journey was filled with magical adventures, but they are to be told another day.

After an arduous yet exciting climb through the blackness of night, with only the plentiful sprinkling of stars to light our way, we arrived at the top for sunrise. How exhilarated I became, watching sky turn from its inky blackness with gleaming white diamonds, to marvelous hues of purple, blue and pink. Soon the glorious sun rose, shedding its light across the magnificent land, setting Africa aglow below us with its host of exquisite and euphoric colors. We had two hours to hike from this point to the actual summit; we walked along the edge of the glaciers that shone like giant white luminous spheres. Exhausted, barely able to take the next step, the high altitude taking its toll, we staggered the last few feet. Every step was worth it though. Despite the fact that my toes were freezing, my fingers numb, I was elated with the achievement and the brilliance of where I was. We collapsed and laughed with joy as we reached the peak. Again I rejoiced in a natural state of ultimate oneness, transcending the separate sense of self. My breath moved as if connected with the whole world, and I looked out from my eyes in silent love. The paranomic view was astounding and spellbinding, and the magic of Kilimanjaro joyously bathed our souls.

Very shortly we began our descent. Here, with my heart so open and so full of gratitude for life, I felt the pain of the world. I was walking behind Sam and our guide when all of a sudden I was filled with an overwhelming feeling that dropped me to my knees, and I cried long sobs. I did not comprehend the emotion; it was again beyond me, more than me. The soul of the planet cried out in pain and I was part of it and it was moving through me. The influx of emotions swathed my being, ephemeral yet powerful. I tried to keep walking but every few minutes I dropped to my knees in tears and pain. I let the ground hold me and I cried, then joy swept through me as I felt God touch me, hold me and caress me with loving. Grief and joy swept through me simultaneaously — a river of life and death it seemed, flowing through my veins and through the veins of the world.

It was a few days later when we were at the bottom of the mountain and took a small plane across the dry, dusty plains of

NEPTUNE'S DAUGHTER

Kenya to our secluded lodge, that we heard the dreadful news of the World Trade Center. Stepping from the plane, we walked a few steps to the waiting jeep and our solemn-looking host shared the heartbreaking news. He had no idea that we did not know about the tragedy that had occurred a week earlier. We were shocked, distressed and heartbroken. The following weeks we continued our adventure in Africa, but experienced deep polarities of emotion. As I walked through the boundless, breathtaking land, observing the awe-inspiring symbiotic relationship between animal, man and earth, I felt a deep respect and inner peace. Yet my heart was also in my homeland, feeling the pain and anguish of apparently unnecessary death and destruction. I would wake up with tears rolling down my cheeks, my dreams full of angst and sadness. Then, looking out from my bed to the open space before me, I watched elephants and gazelle drinking peacefully together at the waterhole, and I recognized the blessings that were bestowed upon me, and upon the Earth.

Like thousands of people around the world, I prayed tirelessly, knowing we have the ability to help heal the pain with our love and compassion. I also joined those on another landscape, who have the unique ability to travel to the other side and assist with transition. We ventured into the scarcely traveled terrain of the human psyche, a spiritual quest of sorts, contributing in our way to a major event in need of so much assistance.

Chapter Twelve

Acquisition of Conscious Awareness

Self trust is the first secret of success.
–Ralph Waldo Emerson

The spirit is the conscious ear.
–Emily Dickenson

S SOON AS I WAS INFORMED about the intriguing class I eagerly signed up. The prospect of working with cadavers that had not been embalmed was appealing and exciting. An opportunity to explore and navigate through the human body, layer by layer, intricately dissecting the sophisticated and highly complex human structure was not to be missed.

The main objective of this class was for cranial practitioners to explore the craniosacral system — all the membranes and tissue that surround the central nervous system and brain — while being able to see first hand how the light touch of a cranial practitioner can have profound effects on the whole body.

The tissue we worked with was still pliable and comparable to living tissue; it had only been about twelve hours since the individuals' death. I was able to apply the lightest touch to the membranes around the brain and see it translate down to the end of the spine. That in itself was enlightening and validating to the power of this profession. After working on the cadaver for some time, I took a short break and thoughtlessly rested my hand upon the chest to watch another girl work. As I concentrated on her delicate exploration of the tissue, I began to have a very peculiar reaction in my hand. Astonished, I quickly jerked my arm away. The sensation of confusion had been oozing into me stemming from the dead man's chest. When I took my hand away the sensation stopped, so curiously, I placed my hand on the chest once again. The same thing happened — I was acutely aware of the sensation of confusion. Quite taken aback, I looked at the chest and realized my hand had been placed on a long thick scar where he had undergone open heart surgery. If indeed the tissue held its own consciousness, it would be feasible that this particular tissue would be confused after such a traumatic event. I began experimenting and placing my hands at different locations of the body. There was an assortment of sensations. Anger emerged from the lung area, and when the chest cavity was cut open and I took out the lungs, I saw the black-stained cells of a heavy smoker. Sadness permeated upward from bladder area, and when I dissected that area, I uncovered numerous surgical procedures. I found it to be quite a disturbing exploration as I continued, unsure what to make of it all. I had just assumed that once one died all consciousness immediately left the body with the soul, and the body that is left is lifeless; yet this did not appear to be so.

I entered a deep place of contemplation. I assumed that the consciousness or energy that was left in the tissue would dissipate into the atmosphere as the body disintegrated, and the soul no longer affected it. So what really interested me was the emotion and sensation that we carry in our bodies while we are still living, while our souls are still occupying the body itself, and what kind of weighty authority it could have over our psyches. Our consciousness, emotions and feelings permeate our whole body; body sensations themselves are often given little thought, and pain becomes a nuisance at the very least. I know I have dissociated from my body and the annoyance of its sensations when they were adverse to me. In the past, it has appeared easier for me to associate with only my ego self, mental personality and self-image. The body is perceived as something that is helpful for activities, yet burdensome in its pain and aging as it disqualifies me from doing everything I want. I have seen people wanting to separate from their bodies, as the body gave them a sense of their mortality, which they did not necessarily want to see. Through the years of conscious exploration, I have experienced an ageless understanding of what the Self is and have become aware of the limiting physical boundaries I set up.

In extending my identity to my whole organism, but not attaching myself to it, I am much more likely to be in touch with what is happening at this gross level and how its effects correlate with my reactions and emotions in daily life. I know I am not my physical body, but I am imbued in it until the body dies and I move on. Released from the belief that we are our body's sensations, emotions and thought processes helps us to dis-identify from them. We can begin to observe them and see how they dissolve, that they are in fact energy moving, dissolving, not who we are at all. Responding with wisdom to our human hindrances, rather than blindly acting, gives us a greater sense of freedom and clearly brings us into the present moment. In the present moment is where the true fruits of life lie.

I had a fascinating experience of being with the body and its sensations at a ten-day Vippassana course. The essence of the teachings in this particular meditation practice is to develop insight. Vippassana is an extraordinarily simple yet profound path to self-awareness that, with continual daily practice, can lead to deep insights and a level of equanimity in daily living that can eventually lead to enlightenment.

I found myself in a very simple environment, at the edge of Yosemite National Park, slightly anxious and observing the dialogue in my own mind of reasons to hastily leave or stay. Meditating for eleven hours a day would certainly be no comparison in hardship to climbing mountains, studying for exams or focusing on intense projects, I reasoned with myself. Yet my ordinary mind and ego were well aware of the anxiety of being alone, focusing only on breath and bodily sensations for the next ten days. Surely I had much more important tasks to be doing. But no — I was here for a reason, and ten days was a relatively short period of time. There was to be no communication with others, two simple meals a day and only the bare necessities for accommodations. I had been looking forward to this experience for quite some time, and the opportunity to be in the environment created for this retreat really was a blessing. I took a breath and made the commitment.

For the first three days the directions were to focus on the sensation occurring at the space between the upper lip and nostrils. I worked diligently, guiding my awareness continuously to the sensations of this area until I found myself able to concentrate without distraction for quite some time. This deep concentration is necessary to further oneself on this path.

On the fourth day I could have cried with joy! Our instructions were changed and I was allowed to shift my attention to other areas of my body. "Hallelujah!" I thought excitedly, trying not to laugh out loud, or cry out "Thank you, thank you!" My upper lip was more familiar to me now than I had ever needed it to be, and almost cared no longer what sensations arose in each moment there. My ordinary mind felt so joyous to have another activity with which to occupy itself. Now I was to move intricately through every area of my body, exploring the reality of mind and matter, aware only of the range of sensations in the area of focus. For an hour I moved from head to toe, meticulously and scrupulously moving over every inch of my body piece by piece, not allowing distraction of thought or more obvious sensations like a fly walking over my forehead, or an annoying itch in my ear, to take me away form the body part of focus.

Soon a shift began to occur in my whole organism. I no longer had gross physical sensations, but rather my body had turned to a field of vibration. It had begun in my hands. I tried to ignore the sensations as I was focusing on my toes, but I was aware of the vibratory sensation quickly moving upward through my arms, chest and torso until my whole body vibrated with a high frequency and I felt like a field of molecules dancing crazily, yet with some inherent order. I experienced my body as it actually is. The sensation was extremely pleasant, yet the instructions are to not become attached to anything that may arise — no desire or craving and no adversity either. Sitting with absolute equanimity with whatever arose in each moment, and as a sensation arose, it did pass and eventually my gross physical body came back into awareness, yet I was left with the insight of the reality of my physical being.

To observe the body sensation without reacting, without attachment, becomes a way to know that we are not that sensation. The pain is not who I am, the anger is not who I am — it is simply a sensation bound to change, and no longer needs to overwhelm or control me. I do not need to suffer because of it, causing and compiling more suffering. Through the practice of Vippassana, awareness of the entire mental-physical structure is gained, as the fence between the subconscious and conscious is broken. What once might have been reaction without thought becomes action performed with a balanced mind. Build up of past emotional blocks begin to disperse through the organism and mind, creating a wonderful lightness and liberating sense of being.

Gestalt Therapy created by Fritz Pearls, is another way to work with emotions within the physical structure. It is an amazing, holistic approach to healing and personal growth in which one can dialogue with one's emotions and body parts. The purpose is to explore polarities, get to know them, accept them and fully appreciate one's complete Self as a whole. Negative or positive aspects of us can dialogue with one another — love and hate, anger and tranquility, aggression and non-violence. Each polarity that arises can be given a voice, expressed in a safe environment, and a state of peace and inner harmony realized. Gestalt Therapy brings one into the here and now, appreciating the body as the home for Spirit while finding a wise and deep spontaneity clear of the ego's consciousness.

With awareness and equanimity our true illuminating nature begins to emerge and the release of suffering is imminent. I imagine that the stored emotions of the body I had been dissecting affected that man's daily life, actions and desires. Why wait until we die to release ourselves from suffering? There are many ways to do this in the here and now, and doing so aids and benefits our communities, country and the planet as a whole.

In the end, the awareness we develop to the minute aspects of life, within and without ourselves, increases the consciousness of all; for we are part of a system in itself that forms part of a greater system and organism. We are in ultimate reality an indivisible whole.

Chapter Thirteen

What is
^a*Dream ?*

> *A man dreams he is a butterfly,*
> *When he wakes up he wonders*
> *Am I a man who dreamt that I am a butterfly*
> *Or am I a butterfly now dreaming I am a man?*
> *–Toaist sage*

I *swam in the vast blue ocean with silky grey dolphins;*
I could feel the cold water rushing against my body
as I jubilantly jumped out and dove back into the
water. Great white sharks swam along beside us, devouring
everything that got in their way. I sensed the power of the
great sharks and the peace and divinity of the dolphins. A
raging fire was burning close to the shore, its flames
leaping menacingly at the water.

The next evening I dreamt again: Great white sharks
were swimming close to the shoreline, again devouring
everything that was before them. The dolphins were
jumping and splashing in the ocean in the distance. I was
on the sand this time, watching the sharks coming closer to
those who were swimming in the shallow waves. I picked
up a burning pole and put the flames to the water, stopping
the atrocious devastation of the destructive sharks.

Fire and water, fire and water — for days I dreamt of these grand archetypal forces coming together, always with symbols of the divine close by. My body was preparing for an immense internal shift. Shortly after these dreams began, a great fire was initiated in my body, always followed by a ruthless coldness, driving stagnant energy out from within me. It was preparing me for an energy awakening that took me to a level of existence beyond time, space and causation.

The rising of potent life-force energy was first appearing in my dreams, before its magnificence rose to my crown, awakening me to the truth. Any concept of a separate sense of self was soon to be obliterated, and I would know eternal bliss existed, even though I still would experience the illusion of separation in my human experience. The truth would remain with me, a perpetual guide, continuing to point me to bring truth into everyday existence. I trust the process of the revelations; the energy moved me into profound meditative stillness, yoga postures and a union with my breath. These paths I continue to walk, knowing they are ancient and primordial ways to connect with our truth and evolution of consciousness.

I recognize that I have different levels of dreams, and different realms in which these take place. There is my mind sorting though the day's thoughts, and there is the level where I meet with others — a school of sorts. I can be gone from my physical body, or deep in the vast space within, exploring other dimensions and experiencing other planes of consciousness. Sometimes I find myself the observer, sometimes the player, or sometimes both at once. I believe there are many layers of reality and dreamtime is an opportunity to explore these. I recognize forgotten parts of my psyche reaching up into my consciousness. I see archetypes, symbols and teachers, receive awesome spiritual teachings, and I receive spiritual guidance.

Symbols and archetypes can be universal, cultural or individual. Looking at symbols in my dreams, I can begin to recognize their significance and teachings, like road maps directing me to my essence. They can also be preparatory as in the dreams I shared in the beginning of this chapter. The phenomenon of dreams can bring so much creative energy into my waking hours when I take the teaching from Tibetan Dream Yoga — to have the experience rather than trying to project my own limiting interpretation on the dream. I do not always do this though; sometimes the dream is so real that I cannot help but dwell on it, or be in the continuous emotions, needing the message to reveal itself. Occasionally I find myself so immersed in the emotional excess of the dream throughout the day, it is as if the dream is not willing to let me go until I face it head on, confronting the experience. As subtle insights reveal themselves, I find teachings that can further me on my path of awakening.

My dreams have proven to be great friends and benefactors, great sources of creativity and fun. Dreams have taught me and led me down colorful avenues of peculiar, insightful adventures.

In the vast and beautiful dimensions that we venture to during the evening hours as we sleep, great mysteries and adventures are ours to behold. How often do we pay attention to our nightly escapades? Our dreams are mostly forgotten as we open our eyes to the daylight hours, if in fact we are able to remember them at all. Although I think most of us at some point in our lives have remarkable, powerful dreams that stay with us — the emotion being so strong it pursues us relentlessly through the day, affecting our waking hours — I do not think it is a typical practice to remember dreams and appreciate their significance in our lives. Nor do most of us realize the powerful potential of a dream, allowing us to move toward liberation, clearing the obscurations of consciousness. What if our dreams were as real as the day, if they were full of profound learning and experience? Or what if our day was as unreal as dreams? Are we the dreamer or the dreamed? Or are we the observer of all of this?

In Tibetan Dream Yoga there is a higher dream practice, more spiritual than psychological, that makes its way below the meaning of the dream, to the core of the dream experience itself. Instead of projecting our own mind's interpretation onto the dream, it is held with reverence, allowing experience and learning to be found, as it can be in our waking hours. One practice is to remain aware while one is dreaming by focusing on particular chakras before falling to sleep. The chakra acts as a gateway to access a particular state of consciousness. Lucidity in the dream is eventually developed, until eventually one can control the dream itself. This generates greater self observation in our waking state, giving us the opportunity to respond, rather than blindly react to any situation.

The practice during the waking hours is to perceive everything as if it were a dream. We can change our emotions as if in a lucid dream, creating flexibility and freeing oneself from the chains of identification with them. Everything is a dream, all encounters are illusory; emotions, judgments, actions — all a dream. The practice also begins to lessen attachment, desire and aversion. Awareness is cultivated throughout the day and night and eventually opens the path to who we truly are, ultimately preparing us also to be "awake" when we die. In learning to observe dreams from the higher state of mind or awareness, as in daily life, it is seen that we are never actually asleep — we are not our thoughts or actions, but everything is a projection of our minds. Who we truly are is the vast awareness that observes, that which is pure cosmic consciousness.

We sleep approximately a third of our lives. I find it exhilarating to be aware for some of this time, or at least remember some periods, and spend a few moments each morning reflecting on my night's journeys, before I let them go. I often write my dreams down, and months or years later take a look back at the extraordinary excursions that took place, delight in the mostly-forgotten adventures, and recognize how the experience was reflecting part of my life.

I am particularly grateful for the dreams that are messages of love, so when I wake in the morning I experience that love. I know I am always being cared for at a higher level than that of my physical existence. I am imbued in the physical, but I am so much more than that. I want to share a very significant dream here as an example of my experiences. I do not recall exactly what was happening in my life at the time, but I recall a sense of hopelessness. I remember the dream very clearly, though, that came to comfort and support me. Archetypal, symbolic, and holding a clear message to have faith, this dream was very powerful:

My partner is Jesus Christ; he is tall with lengthy light brown hair, wearing a long, soft white robe. Peace and love emanate from his whole being. I am experiencing his love in my whole body, but especially in my heart. This is where I feel the core of unconditional love. We are holding each other, my arms tightly around him. It is as if I am afraid to let go, for he may disappear. I cannot let go of this love. In the next image I am waiting for him to come, but he does not show up. I had to struggle to find faith: in my belief of him, of his love for me, that he was with me even when he was not physically there. Eventually he did come back. He smiled at me, unperturbed by my foolish emotions. It came to me that I had to let go of my ideas and the fear I was grasping onto causing me so much suffering; I needed to have complete faith and to experience this exquisite love that was larger than I.

In my dream, I remember barely being able to contain the enormous love in my body, and the feeling woke me up, my body gently vibrating with gentle streams of energy. I understood the message to have faith; that I am always loved, never forgotten, and even when I feel alone and hopeless, this is an illusion of my ordinary mind.

Sleep can bring a rather alarming phenomenon, sleep paralysis, which is a bizarre happening that occurs during the night. The first experience of sleep paralysis in my adult life, (I was about twenty-three), was accompanied by an intense vibration, a definite presence and an apparition that was witnessed not only by me but by my partner.

As I lay sleeping in bed, a vibration disturbed me from my dreams. The high frequency of this vibration startled me. As I tried to move, I realized I could not! My eyelids would not open, my body was stiff and heavy. I was completely paralyzed! I expanded my consciousness outward, sensing the room around me, as I could not see or move, and I quickly became aware of a heavy presence on the bed beside me. It was this presence that was causing the incredibly fast vibration.

"Take a deep breath," I thought, "and then call for Steve." As I felt myself take a deep breath, my body jolted. Immediately I could move and the vibration and heaviness that was beside me on the bed disappeared. Or had it?

Steve, my boyfriend, came rushing into the bedroom and I told him what had happened.

"What do you think it was? How do you feel now?" He asked, rapt by my story.

"I don't know what it was, but I have a really strange pressure on the inside of my forehead. There's pressure on the inside of my throat and my stomach too. I'm feeling nauseous."

I was experiencing a very strange and unfamiliar sensation throughout my whole body. This pressure was emanating outward from inside of me, especially around the areas of my chakras. As I explained this to Steve, I suddenly expressed an overwhelming feeling. "Oh my God, something is inside me!" Startled at my words, we both laughed.

This was the only way I could describe the peculiar pressure from within, though. The statement was as odd to me as it may sound, but that was the experience. My mind reflected back to the moment my body jolted. Could it be that whatever was beside me on the bed somehow jumped inside me? My rational mind said no. My intuition on the other hand, gave me the distinct impression that something else was populating my physical body.

After some contemplation, and a discussion about what to do, we came up with an idea. "Ask whatever it is to leave. Something like this happened to me in New York," my other roommate offered. He had joined Steve and I in the curious conversation.

"I didn't have anything inside me, but I felt a definite presence in the room that was frightening. I demanded it leave, and as soon as I said that a cold wind blew through the room and it left. Very weird. I'll never forget that," John continued, scratching his head as he remembered.

It was unlike John to talk about such things, so I thought I would give it a try. We could not think what else to do. I gingerly walked over to our full-length mirror in the small hallway. I stood looking at myself, feeling rather foolish. Curious, compassionate, and always fascinated, Steve stood behind me in the bedroom doorway. Our eyes met in the mirror and he smiled encouragingly. These things were out of his range of knowledge and experience, as well as mine, but he always remained open and captivated in unusual situations. Sheepishly I began to talk, still feeling a little silly, yet my other roommate encouraged me to do so. "If it was a spirit it will respond to your request," John assured me. I was glad he had suddenly become knowledgeable of the paranormal. I shrugged my shoulders, not thinking anything would actually happen. Yet I continued talking in front of the full length mirror, feeling a little silly.

"If there is any spirit within in me, show yourself." Nothing happened. "If anything is inside me show yourself, and if you're not friendly you should leave immediately." I stood motionless for a moment before I began to gently vibrate, my eyes widened in disbelief. Thoughts of the movie *The Exorcist* passed through my mind and I quickly decided, "You should leave no matter what." The situation was extremely eerie, yet the bizarre sensations I was having were getting stronger. Then my voice changed; a deep and unusual resonance chilled me. Steve was beginning to look alarmed.

"Whatever you are, show yourself right now," I demanded in the strange deep voice. And so it did!

In the mirror a startling apparition appeared. I could barely believe it. An old woman stood before me. She had almond-shaped eyes, and could have been American Indian or Asian. She had actually moved outward from my body, standing a few inches in front of me. Although I could not feel her physically, she was positively there, her reflection in the mirror continuing to astound me. Her skin was extremely wrinkled, and there was the dignified wisdom of age on her face, yet she was expressionless, as her ghostly eyes gazed into mine. I was not as surprised as Steve who was watching this intently from behind me. I shifted my eyes from her for a moment and looked at him. The bewildered expression on his face assured me he was witnessing this too. My gaze went back to the old woman. We stood in silence for a few more moments, wide-eyed and mesmerized with her ghostly image and presence. She was pale and ethereal, so I could not see any color or definite outlines but for her face, and she was about four inches shorter than I. I could feel my heart racing excitedly in the midst of the unexpected revelation. After a period of about thirty seconds — quite a while, considering — she shifted slowly back into my body. I remained calm yet stupefied as I digested the unusual encounter. I sensed no hint of malevolence, nor was I frightened. The nausea and pressure lessened and I did not feel invaded even though I knew then someone, or something else, was taking up residence in my body. This rather precarious situation demanded some silence from me.

"Oh my God!" Steve exclaimed. "That was amazing! Who is she; where did she come from? . . . Julie, what's going on?" Steve asked a bit concerned about me, as I looked a little pale.

"I have no idea," I replied after a few moments.

"Has she gone?"

"No, I still feel her inside of me. I'm feeling really tired, I'm going to bed!"

"You can't just go to sleep!" Steve said.

I thought for a moment. "Yes I can." I was too tired and the mysterious woman had ignited a need for reflection. A spirit had entered my body, she was still there, and this defied any previous beliefs I had held or even thought about.

"I'll meditate for a while. Maybe she's my spirit guide or maybe it is me in spirit form, or maybe she's just passing by. I'm sure it's going to be okay."

I did meditate for a short while and said a prayer before falling into a deep sleep. In the morning when I woke, there was no sensation of pressure, and I was sure whoever-she-was had gone. I was left again with having experienced something I could not explain, outside the realm of the tangible world. But it certainly opened me up to possibilities that I had not considered before. I decided it might be a good idea to create some sort of protecting shield. I imagined a large circular shield around me, glowing white and emanating love. I asked for protection from my guides and teachers and for the shield to always be around me.

I never experienced another being inside me that I felt did not belong, but I did meet many along my travels as a spiritual adventurer. I experienced sleep paralysis quite a few more times, sometimes sensing or seeing shadowy figures moving about me. At times I felt myself paralyzed inside of a dream. My favorite, which I remember so well and hold close to my heart, was a dream of who I now think of as my angel, Michael.

I was surrounded by darkness, unable to move and I was frightened. I was aware I was dreaming, but I could not wake up. I felt stuck in some awful place of fear and darkness. "What can I do?" I thought. It felt like something was chasing me. I was trying desperately to run, but could barely move my body. I was suspended in this horrible, dark place without a way out.

"Wake up, wake up," I pleaded with myself, aware I was dreaming, but still I was not able to. I felt hopeless, and my last effort to escape from the darkness that held me was to gather as much energy and effort as I possibly could and scream.

"MICHAEL!" My scream shattered the blackness and I astonished myself with the name I had called out. I did not know any Michael.

*As soon as the scream left my lips, I was instanta-
neously in a beautiful garden. I was surrounded by lush
green trees, and blossoming fragrant flowers draped from
the vibrant plants. I looked upward to a balcony on my left,
and saw a beautiful man standing there watching me,
smiling affectionately. Michael. He was not at all surprised
to see me. His bright eyes were filled with compassion as he
gazed lovingly at me. His wise and handsome face was
adorned with a short beard and his long, dark hair hung
softly down to his shoulders. Radiant energy glowed all
around him.*

*"Do not be afraid Julie. I am always with you." His
words reached my heart and I experienced his unconditional love and acceptance.*

*"Yes, he is always with me." I knew this. "There is
never anything to be afraid of." I was filled with joy and
peace.*

The Eden-like garden slowly faded and I opened my eyes.
I lay still in my bed reflecting. This was beyond a dream; it was
real and a great gift. I could still feel the wonderful love, my
heart was open, and I knew ultimately that there was nothing to
fear. Fear was of my own making, and from the making of
human consciousness as it identifies itself as flesh. It is unable to
really hurt me. Fear, of course, is also a great benefactor. It is a
primary survival instinct, and a natural emotion for us to
observe and respond to. Rather than allowing fear to rule us,
however, we can learn to distinguish the difference between
instinctive and psychological fear, just as we do with other
emotions. In recognition of fear, rather than allowing it to
encompass me, I learned to face it, and not identify with it.

Waking up in the night or early morning, one can find oneself completely paralyzed, only able to move the eyes. Scientifically it is unknown what actually occurs, and in my research I found a few hypotheses that discuss the mechanisms of the brain, yet no definitive answers. Occasionally, sleep paralysis can be part of a sleeping disorder called Narcolepsy, which is identified usually because of severe daytime sleepiness and Cataplexy, in which partial or complete muscle weakness occurs, triggered by a strong emotion. Yet what the sleep paralysis is, remains a mystery.

The paralysis is often accompanied by what is medically known as hypnagogic hallucinations. A hallucination is defined as "an apparent perception of an external object when no such object exists." In these "hallucinations," people often become very frightened, seeing strange entities or ghosts wandering around, sometimes touching or sitting on them! These so-called hallucinations are not always visual. Auditory experiences can also occur. Usually a buzzing or vibrating sound accompanies sleep paralysis that can be quite loud and disturbing. I thought it was interesting that the same phenomena of buzzing, high-pitched vibrations and unusual noises occur when the fifth Chakra is activated. Visions and the ability to see the spirit world are related to the opening of the sixth chakra, know as the third eye or inner vision.

I read an interesting story about a Canadian physicist who had been having sleep paralysis for a number of years and feared his condition until he read an article from a Japanese psychologist. This article stated that sleep paralysis is a brief stage of sleep when the brain is "disconnected" from the body. It went on to say that the brain is semi-asleep so the person cannot move, and often sees shadowy figures, as the eyes may be open. The physicist was thankful that his condition was "diagnosed" by science at a time that is not so superstitious, fearing he may have been labeled as mentally ill not so long ago. It struck me as odd that the experiences could then be dismissed so easily without any real or substantial explanation of what is actually happening. "What diagnosis?" I thought.

It appears that sleep paralysis is more common than we think, and for the same reason as this physicist, people are afraid to talk about such unusual events, fearing they may be classed as psychotic or a little crazy. This is such a prevailing attitude in society — fear of being stigmatized with a pathological label. While sleep paralysis is not indicative of any psychological problem, it continues to be a little taboo to talk about mysterious events of the night. These mysteries will never be revealed to us if we continue to suppress and hide from them. Our souls are thirsty for us to reveal ourselves. I can no longer squelch my dancing spirit and hide from the truth. Even if I have to plunge down into the darker reaches of my being, I am willing to share and explore the possibilities. I know changes can be real and permanent as I integrate my learning into my present reality.

The changes are tangible, my life is continuously renewing in exciting ways and I know nothing happens without meaning or purpose. As I began to talk to people about such events, most people had experienced sleep paralysis at least once. They remembered the episode very clearly and found some peace in just being able to talk about it, knowing they were not the only ones to experience this, and acknowledged they would not be scared if it happened again. I think this is exciting. Fear can be so inhibiting and limiting; yet it is the energy that is compounded by something we are afraid of that needs to come to light. I have also explained how fear can draw to it negative energies that feed on fear to continue its cycle. To allow fear to run its course, allow it to dissipate, as we neutrally observe, can free us from its bondage.

Sometimes it may feel so frightening that we are going to die, yet it is the resistance that dies and the fear itself, not who we are.

I have experienced sleep paralysis many times, in various circumstances and know the visions are no mere "hallucination." I remembered having dreams as a child and feeling paralyzed. I learned to pull in as much air as possible, then let it out trying to form any sound I could. This usually would pull me from whatever force was holding me and I would wake up. I do not remember being frightened; I just lay and my curious child's mind would wonder for a while, and then forget about it.

Another paralysis story I would like to share happened the morning I returned from India, in September of 2000. I was thirty-three.

The return journey from India was exhausting — twenty-four hours of flying. I slept a few hours on each flight, but when I eventually got home I was really tired. Luckily it was evening and at 7:30 PM I went to sleep not waking until 5:00 AM. I wanted to see if I could sleep a few more hours and prevent jet lag so I tried to go back to sleep. My mind was not quiet. Thoughts about Sai Baba, whose ashram I had just visited, floated melodiously around my mind. I was sad to have left India and the sacredness of my journey, but so grateful for the time there. I tossed and turned in bed for a while and eventually decided to read a book about Sai Baba, determined not to get up so early. I read a few pages, felt my eyes get heavy and was able to fall back to sleep.

Unsure how much later it was, I awoke with cold fiercely pulling me from my sleep. My feet felt like icicles. I got up and put on some woolen socks and got back into bed. The cold was intense and seemed determined to make me suffer. Maybe I was getting sick, I thought, but intuitively I knew I was not. I could not remember being so cold before. Getting up again I piled two more blankets on the bed. Lying there, swathed in my blankets, I could feel the cold rising up my legs; it was very unusual, like an internal chilling entity seeping up through me, seizing my body for itself. I thought again that I may be getting sick, as the sensation was so strange. Yet other than the icy chill, I felt fine. I noticed the room was not cold, and September in Southern California just does not get this nippy. "What is going on?" I wondered. Eventually the cold had risen up from my legs and had consumed my whole body. I was freezing and very sleepy now. The cold and tiredness took me and I drifted off to sleep. Maybe an hour later I woke up very hot. I kicked off my socks and extra blankets. I was scorching! I lay listless, with the heat becoming more intense. Burning from inside me, my spine felt like it was on fire. Did I have a virus? Was my body trying to fight it off with heat? I did not feel sick though, but something abnormal was going on. The heat intensified, especially in my lower spine, but I was not sweating — so weird, I remember thinking. My insides were feeling like an inferno and the flames were licking up and down my spine. I was going to call for Sam, who was upstairs, but the heat was so consuming I was unable to summon any energy to call. I lay there for a while in a stupor, wondering if I would die and be found later with my insides peculiarly scorched. Maybe I was going to spontaneously combust; there was a lightness of heart about it all, though, as I experienced myself going through this unusual journey. Whatever this was though, was deeply connected with my spine.

Thankfully I fell back into sleep. I am not sure what it was that woke me, but when I became conscious I was entirely paralyzed. I could sense where my body was; I was lying on my left side, with my eyes almost closed, my arms in front of me, and my fingers in front of my face. I tried to move them. I put all my effort and concentration into moving them, but they would not budge. My eyelids stayed stubbornly still too, but there was a gap and I could just see through my eyelashes to my fingers. Movement around me caught my attention, and I thought Sam must be there, moving around the bed. But there was someone else there, too.

"Who is in my bedroom with Sam?" I wondered. I tried to move to attract attention, to let Sam know my spine was on fire, and that something bizarre was happening to me, but still my body would not respond. I could see the shadowy figures clearer now, moving around me as I peeked out from the gap in my eyelids. They were walking back and forth around the bed, placing things on the bedside table.

"That's unusual, we don't have bedside tables," I thought. And although I could not see any tables, it seemed as if that's what they were doing. I knew I was awake, and I knew then it was not Sam, but at least two spirits seemingly tending to me. I watched their shadowy presence for awhile, the consuming heat still rising up my spine, and I could only lie there and wait. I felt affectionately cared for; the tenderness that filled me came from those around me. Upstairs, I heard the doorbell ring and after a few moments heard Sam talking to his assistant. How I wished he would come down and see this, if he could. I was helpless and fascinated as I lay there. It came to me I was experiencing kundalini energy. There was a high-pitched ringing in my ears and the hot flames sparked and cascaded up my spine in a strange, pulsating rhythm. After a short while I fell back into sleep.

I woke up and my temperature felt normal. I could move but I was incredibly exhausted. I lay there on my bed, fatigued and dazed, until Sam eventually walked in. His assistant had just left, and he was coming down to check on me. It was about ten o'clock. He looked curiously at me for a moment, my face was drawn and my complexion pale.

"Are you okay?" Sam asked a little concerned.

"Were you in here a little while ago?" I asked, although I knew he had not been.

"No, I've been working. Sheilenna came by with some papers for me to sign. She just left and I thought I'd better come see if you were awake yet. It's ten o'clock."

I slowly recounted what I had been through. We sat in silence for a while. It was not a dream, or delirious illusions, but something real. Kundalini is the potent life force that resides in the lower spine or sacrum. Often people who visit spiritual teachers have a powerful experience of kundalini energy rising, so this was a possible and likely explanation after seeing Sai Baba. I felt that the two energy beings were working on my subtle energy body. The powerful rising of kundalini was overwhelming for my energetic circuits, and so I received help from the spirit world.

Over the next few weeks, I had periods of intense happiness and joy, strange vivid dreams filled my nights, and a new lovely energy filled my days. I felt high on life, and in love with everything. I experienced and noticed this new way of being for a couple of months before it faded, or integrated naturally into my life. What remained was the innate experience of connectedness. As the eternal energy rose through me, it awakened my internal senses. My consciousness was heightened, my attitude toward myself and others brightened with the knowing that this energy is part of us all.

We can all awaken this intelligence within, it is our natural energy flow; yoga is one way, or visualizing and working with the chakras. There are plentiful meditations that will invariably fill us with love, light and inner harmony. The final outcome is reunion with God, as we rediscover our true nature, and realize the dream.

"Wake up! You are already free"
–Sri H. W. L. Poonjaji
"Your true nature is happiness and bliss."
–Ramana Maharishi.

Chapter Fourteen

Dynamic Stillness

All things in fact begin to change their nature and appearance;
one's whole experience of the world is radically different....
There is a new vast and deep way of experiencing, seeing,
knowing, contacting things.
–Sri Aurobindo

If you observe well, your own heart will answer.
–de Lubilz

MEDITATION IN ITS MANY FORMS is a wonderful path to awakening. I have studied different techniques and deeply resonated with a few that have given me a sturdy framework to contain my experiences. Meditation can be silent and still, where I move into a vast awareness, or it can take me to experiences that are beyond my imagination — mythical, symbolic and very real. I can move beyond the physical realm to subtler energy systems of myself and the universe. I can find an intelligent purpose behind the experiences of the physical realm, helping me meet the daily challenges life can bring. I begin to see the patterns and habits that have run my life, and begin to break free from there binding constraint. Through resting in awareness of what is present in each moment, meditation can open up the truth of our original nature — or what is called original mind, in Buddhism. Daily life can change as I develop more clarity, awareness and recognition of what is happening in each moment. Mystical encounters have opened my heart with delightful symbols that have birthed new possibilities and compassion deep within me.

One may be still, concentrate deeply, rest in awareness, chant, repeat a mantra, or decide to venture inward on a sacred journey of the heart. All help to quiet the mind, keeping one present in each moment. Meditation is not passive; it is not about relaxation but making the mind receptive to reality. Thought processes are subdued, so true, original nature can emerge in its shimmering truth. It is important not to chase the mystical, or crave magical encounters. Life is founded in mystery, the mystery of being. Presence in everyday existence, enjoying the flow of our creative energies is a precious gift of meditation. Finding a path and staying on it, through the peaks and the plummets is important, along with faith in the process and a motivation that will continue to propel you on your own journey.

During a meditation where I chose to repeat the mantra "Om Namah Shivaya," which translates to "Honoring the Divine within," I learned about the potential and power a mantra can bring, as well as the potential of what lies within myself.

As I quietly began to repeat the sacred words, my body and mind relaxed as I moved into deep concentration. My physical body changed its gross feeling to a subtler vibration until I had lost all notion of bodily sense. I did not know where my body was in time or space. I knew I was sitting in lotus posture on the floor, for that's where I had physically put myself, but I had lost the impression of my body. I witnessed this from afar as I continued chanting, deeply involved now in the words and meditation, not allowing myself to become distracted by the vibrations. I was enjoying the beginning of euphoric space and expansion as it grew within me.

Gradually I became aware of an eerie, high-pitched noise beyond the silence of my words. Before me, from within, I saw my inner vision gently open, revealing a large, circular, spinning saw. I was slightly surprised, but stayed calm and immersed in the mantra ignoring my mind's curiosity. The saw was coming right at me. About four feet in diameter, the saw was revolving at high speed, the rough edges appearing smooth as it spun speedily with intent, getting closer and closer. Witnessing and experiencing something in a meditative state can be uncanny, as the reality of what is occurring is as real as normal waking state, if not more so. When I experience space around me, it is mostly black with an illuminating quality, but when my inner vision opens, I experience it just like opening my eyes. I see clearly, so to see a large spinning saw was a bit shocking, but in this meditative state I am the witness, so there is no evaluation of what is happening. I can watch as I experience, and I know I am safe, yet my mind can be unsure, for there is still duality in this particular state. My mind held on, and I noticed its pull toward the drama, yet I just watched that and did not become a "doer."

I continued repeating the words calmly, aware of a slight anxiety building within, but knowing that is not who I am. I kept going deeper and deeper, instinctively knowing to stay immersed in the mantra, feeling it resonate inside me. The saw continued to move closer, quite relentless, inching its way nearer. I continued to witness from a higher spiritual perspective as the next few moments unfolded before me, feeling myself move closer to the eternal witness and not a separate self. My body came back into my awareness, but it was not my own body, but a hard black and red shell in the form of Buddha.

"Om Namah Shivaya, Om Namah Shivaya," I repeated, absorbing myself in the resonating energy of the chant, watching, feeling, experiencing. Just inches away from me now, I knew the saw was about to strike me, so real my mind desperately wanted to break free and run. My mind shivered with trepidation, the noise now louder and louder, ringing in my inner ear, until it reached the hard outer shell of my form. The high pitch of the saw screeched loudly as it touched me and began cutting through the black and red form.

"Om Namah Shivaya, Om Namah Shivaya," I chanted over and over, staying connected. The anxiety heightened, my mind trying to pull me out of this intense mantra, but I was determined to stay with myself and disconnect from my mind. Finding courage and inner strength, I stayed with the 'I am' witness. The sharp blade was cutting right through me. Could I actually be cut in half? Here I was, and it was happening. I was spellbound as the saw disappeared behind me. My hard outer shell fell apart, crashing and shattering to the floor beside me into a thousand pieces, exposing a brilliant golden inner luminosity.

I was a beautiful, radiantly shining, golden Buddha. I was in awe, feeling astounded and exhilarated as this wonderful God within was exposed. At the same time, I just was, without judgment — exactly what I saw. I had transcended my physical being. I could see and sense every detail of the golden effigy. Overflowing with peace, I felt calm and pure, as I sat in an erect, still posture. I was conscious of warm tears rolling down my golden cheeks. I continued with the mantra. Deep compassion, love, gratitude, and acceptance of this miraculous experience reverberated through me. I remained calm, peaceful and detached, until the meditation naturally drew to a close. I breathed deeply into my heart, my own body returned now to my senses, as the Golden Buddha softly faded. I was enthralled and deeply moved by this revelation.

The effect of this profound and euphoric experience nourished my inner self. I was left with a deeper sense of compassion and commitment to bring this peace and fulfillment into everyday existence, so that becomes a part of my journey, peace within and peace without.

For me the Buddha signified the archetype of wholeness that he personified. I believe we all have Buddha nature or wholeness within us, ever-present to be awakened. The enchanting and awesome experience of this magical time was a glimpse of what I strive for in my life. I looked to the story of the Buddha to find meaning and direction and found renewed vigor for my life.

Meditation has given me many gifts relative to this reality. The exquisite attentiveness to the moment can capture delicious insights as well as thought-provoking challenges later on. A wonderful, creative force flows freely within, teeming with ideas, knowing and possibilities for patterning my life. Then it is up to me to make the choices. For life is a series of choices, and if we choose wisely, enlightenment will dawn. Meditation brings so much in the way of peace and awareness to my life, and gives me a deeply intuitive knowing. I regard it as an essential part of my day. I do not always have such a profound visual and sensation-filled experience; it is enough just to sit in quietude. Often it is the stillness and quietness of meditation that fills me and balances me with peace. From the beautiful empty space I find myself in, true creativity and insights emerge.

Through the metaphysical events that happen to me, I can see life playing out from a different angle. I see the treasure of life — it becomes richer and laced with more meaning. By allowing the unusual events to unfold without getting caught in attachment of them, I learn how to be present in the moment, capturing the essence and magic of each day. Henry Miller said, *"Until we accept the fact that life itself is founded in mystery, we shall learn nothing."* I resonate so well with this.

I have also found a whole new perspective to what is important to me — experiences of the heart. My experiences and meditation continue to open me up at the heart level in everyday existence. I feel more immersed in life at every level — physical, emotional, spiritual and mental — with an underlying compassion for all sentient beings. I cannot explain all the spiritual mysteries that occur to me, but I know that mysteries are plentiful and continuous in each person's everyday life, including yours.

The beautiful alignment of my body, mind and spirit, is so delicious and delightful it is something I encourage everybody to find time for. We all have Buddha nature. Dwell for a while in the stillness of your own magnificent being. Experience the mysteries within yourself. The space within is full of potentiality, truth and divine love, we can bring forth from this place the magnificence of our being, and manifest it within this reality.

Chapter Fifteen

To Eternity
and Back

*There is a time for everything and a season for every activity
under heaven, a time to be born and a time to die.*
–Ecclesiastes 3:1

A PROFOUNDLY ENLIVENING AND TRULY enlightening day
began on an earnest quest for truth — a time to
know surrender. I could feel my heart longing, a
tiredness and an urgency that was difficult to articulate. I did
not know this day would unveil the greatest illusion and reveal
to me that I need not look elsewhere but inward to quench the
longing.

Everything is already here, we are already enlightened. We
are one with God, pure cosmic energy. We need only to awaken.
The unfolding story has an element of surprise; it was
surprising to me as I came home to myself. The words I declare
in utter amazement are authentic cries of wonder. It is not who
I am, but who we all are.

In my final week of class studying spiritual psychology, the
phrases, "Go deeper, let go, and surrender," were spoken quite
frequently in our process work. I understood these conceptually, of course, and had in fact experienced them in process in
class, as well as in body work and the emotional release work I
had done over the years. After school though, I found myself in

deep contemplation of the ultimate expression, if there was one, of going deeper, letting go and surrendering. And so I found myself one sunny morning at home sitting for my meditation, pondering these words. I began sitting on my firm bed, looking out to the lush green canyon and blue Pacific that shimmered so peaceful and inviting. As if lured by the beauty of nature, I focused on my breath, and decided to journey to the lower world, for an internal journey. Nothing could have prepared me for the extent of this fantastic adventure to my Self.

Inner journeys are rich and spontaneous. As the inner dimensions of my mind open up, a world is portrayed before me that is experienced with the clarity of a movie. I am an active player, unknowing what is to be revealed. Not my imagination, nor a visualization, it is a real mystical, sensory experience happening as I sit in stillness with my eyes closed.

It was not long before I found myself sitting with a small tribe of Native American Indians. This had become my only reality now. There were six of us sitting in a small, enclosed circle around a fire that appeared to have been burning for some time. Evening was drawing near, and the flickering light of the flames danced on our faces, casting an eerie glow. There was an ambience of sacredness, obvious ceremony and expectation. I was handed the long ritual pipe. The shadows danced excitedly about us, knowing the secrets of what was to come, silently laughing at my naïveté. Anxiety began to rise up in me; a thought to flee passed through me, but had little effect. I was deeply involved in the ceremony, as if I had already committed to partake in the holy rites. I sensed the complexity and the deep respect for this ritual. With hand gestures from an old and wise Indian, I was encouraged to take a puff of the pipe. I brought the long burning stick to my lips and sucked the sweet smoke deep into my lungs. The shadows were dancing faster now, "Let go," they whispered softly. "Let go."

I was to take the pipe three times. All eyes were on me, their faces holding the most sober expressions. I searched their eyes for some semblance of reassurance, and I realized I was to take this journey alone. I could feel the warmth of the fire before me, and saw the shadows dancing wildly around us, as the rhythmic drumming filled my ears. The enchanting beat captured and allured me to its magic. I let the sounds take me away as I inhaled for the third time. The still faces kept watching me without expression. I exhaled and felt myself falling backward into the pervading abyss. Deeper and deeper I fell, letting go until one final surrender, the last breath drawn from me as I let the space encompass and embrace me. I lost consciousness in its radiant silence.

It must have been this time that I actually fell out of my sitting meditation on the bed. I had been so deep and involved in the ritual, I was surprised to find myself semi-conscious in the bedroom and not actually in an Indian ceremony. The only body part I could feel now was my left arm — a bizarre and unnerving experience, as it seemed to have been struggling to hold on to its own consciousness, until that too surrendered and faded away. My body became a silhouette of soft vibrations. I wanted to get up, yet I did not, or maybe I could not. I sensed people moving around me, floating above me, talking and whispering. It was too vague for me to hear, but they were discussing me. This was serious; they were concerned. Were they arguing? And still I heard my thoughts, "Go deeper, let go, let go," swooning about me, like a distant signal reminding me, guiding me so I could surrender again; a warm wave of emptiness swept over my mind, melting me like soft snow and I was gone again into the depth of vastness within.

I was dying: I was aware I was dying, and before me my life unfurled. A beautiful, sweet garden of images, soaked with the essence of my life in its entirety. It was most superb to die, the ultimate release of letting go, everything so perfect now. I really believe this is what it will be like to die, for this is what occurred; everything I have ever done will be exquisitely and empathetically seen over.

I was compassion, love, knowing, and in relationship to the divine as I watched scenes of my life replay before me. I was re-experiencing it all, a celebration of life, until everything faded away. I remember only small fragments now, myself as a child, a teenager, connecting with friends, friends dying, family, strangers and an abundance of moving emotions swirling and unfolding. I imagine if I remembered all of it the dramatic impact on my life would be too huge. To know intricately, the reason for every moment of past life would be huge. Although this particular part of the experience is a distant memory for me now, the impact has marked me in a profound way: every moment must have purpose — every choice and action, too. At the end of it all I believe it is me, my own soul, who sees how well I have done in fulfilling its desire, and if I need to come and do it over again.

After my apparent death, death of my ego-consciousness, all was empty. Unknowing how long I floated in emptiness, I still lay on my bed, but eventually I awoke again on an internal plane and I found myself on a dusty red road, in the middle of an expansive, dry red desert. I was surprised to be here in this strange land, confused and lost, no awareness of myself in meditation. This again was the only reality now. The sky above was orange, and a few red clay buildings stood, looking old and abandoned. An old crone, dressed in ragged clothes, was bent over her walking stick, her face deeply lined, laughing mockingly at me. She lifted the stick, her dark glaring eyes peering right at me as if to say I was a fool, and she pointed the way. Her laughter evaporated as her image disappeared and there was again emptiness.

Sometime during my experience, Sam had come into the room to "check on me," as I had been meditating quite some time. As he entered the room and saw me lying on the bed he instinctively stopped with an uneasy apprehension. Looking at my face, fear slowly began to rise in him. My face was unusually pale yet glowing ominously, my eyes were half open, exposing only white. My eyelids were fluttering wildly, and my facial muscles twitching out of control. Later, Sam reflected to me his experience of me during this meditation.

"You looked like a beautiful, crazed goddess. If serpents were squirming from your head, it would not have surprised me!" he said, half joking. "You were obviously in a deep trance and bathed by luminous energy. I was drawn to look especially at your head, where the energy was enormous, and I barely recognized you. I knew a huge energetic current was flowing through you. It was the energy and its power that caused me to silently leave the room, like a cat backing cautiously away to safety. I knew something profound was occurring. I had faith in you to handle your journey," he said. "And with the power emanating from you, rousing fear and caution in me, I was almost too scared to approach. I knew there was little for me to do, but leave the room and sit outside and wait. I thought you might have been having a kundalini opening. I trusted your inherent knowledge of these things."

I do not know how long I was there, lying on my bed, but eventually I returned to a conscious state. I was confused; I felt my mind scrambling to organize itself. "Who was I, where am I, did I die, am I dead?" Images flashed before me — Indians, the old crone, my life, Sam. Where was Sam? I sat up and took in the room. A veil had seemingly dissolved, revealing the deeper delights of what ordinarily may seem like everyday. Everything was glowing anew, vibrating with such vigor that all appeared to be celebrating life. The enchanting room held me for a while before I stood up and, wobbly on my feet, staggered to the door out into the living room. Sam was lying on the sofa and without thought I was right there next to him, waking him.

Before I go on, I feel it is important to explain that what followed next came after experiencing a death of my separate sense of self, or the ego. The sense of "I am" in the normal sense, had dissolved, leaving me with an unusual boundless truth of our deepest reality of who or what is experiencing the individual "I am." There is a unanimous declaration amongst spiritual teachers of all ages that we can come to know God through meditation. Through direct experience I was to reach the state of consciousness in which I was in conscious union with the ultimate reality. I use the term God. This is also my understanding to be Cosmic Consciousness, Allah, Christ Consciousness and many more. An experience that is all of our birthright, the beauty and undeniable experience of one's true Self is ecstatically blissful, to say the least.

"Sam," I cried. His eyes opened, startled by my cry. "I'm God!"

In that moment the realization of what I said echoed around the room, filling me with bliss and exquisite joy. I began laughing and laughing, the sounds wildly coursing through me at my own outrageous revelation.

"Sam, I'm God, I'm God." I sang out, "I'm God realizing I'm Julie realizing I'm God!"

Sam looked so bewildered at my exuberance and surprising

words. Later he told me, "At one level I was not surprised; I believed you and shared your joy, knowing something incredible had taken place. In retrospect, I'm surprised I accepted so readily." I threw my arms about him with love and, incredibly, I merged completely with his body. I was ecstatic. I was experiencing the man that I love so deeply at the most profound and intimate level possible. We became one. We held each other closely, yet I could not define where I ended or he began. There were no boundaries, no separation. I was Sam, he was God, this was bliss. I became Sam. I became his thoughts and feelings; his divine essence and humanness, purely God's exquisite expression. I felt his confusion and questioning, as well as his joy of my excitement. Everything was God creating, expressing for the first time a new and glorious moment of creation. Each thought, feeling and emotion was God.

We released the embrace. I was amazed, so joyful. God experiencing Julie realizing she was God, God ecstatic in these moments of revelation; and Julie, I, continuing to explore in my awakened state. I skipped outside to feel the grass and became the grass — grass consciousness, how I loved to be grass! I knew then I could experience my ultimate dream. What I yearn for so deeply, could be possible. I often sit in meditation or just in appreciation of my surroundings. As I look out to the ocean I feel a longing to merge, to be a part of it, but I am always separate. I often feel sad as I experience this; it is as if I remember a time of connection long, long ago. I knew today this illusion of separation would be gone. I could fulfill the longing that I carry inside me, at last my heartfelt longing.

I looked out to the gleaming blue ocean until I was the vast body of consciousness. I was currents of motion, the ecstatic ocean dance. Dolphins and whales, immense schools of fish, intelligence experiencing life. I was a huge creature swimming at the deepest depths of my ocean body, lonely in the darkness and silence of the deep. Tiny microscopic creatures were an important part of the continuum of the creation, and slight movements of one cell amoebas vastly exquisite. And overhead I flew as the hawk, circling out from the canyon, riding the rippling currents, gracefully moving with the wind, allowing it, me, to take me to the canyon where I stood as a deer, always alert, eating the soft dewy grass.

Drawing myself into the experience of the physical body I could barely contain myself. I was on my knees with gratitude and joy. I crawled back into the house where I clambered up onto a big chair and became catatonic with bliss. An extraordinary feeling of unconditional love was streaming forth from my chest, pulsating in every cell of my body. I had never felt love of this magnitude. My body was vibrating so highly I thought surely if I moved I would combust, exploding in a billion fragments of bliss, but I could not move, nor did I want to. I was pure cosmic love, and it was feeling itself in every cell of my being.

I sat there for hours and when I found I could think, rather than only being, I began to further my discoveries with this new state of consciousness.

I thought of my mother and how I loved her. The escalation of love as I brought her to mind was exquisite. I had a thought of wanting to embrace her with this feeling, but simultaneously I realized that it is she who is always embracing me with love. I am continuously encapsulated, protected by her aura, the exquisite Mother energy. I experienced a soft humbleness as I saw this. How could I ordinarily be so blind in life?

I understood then the power of the ego — how it struggles to hold us in our erroneous beliefs, how desperately it needs to delude us from truth for its own survival. And how I laughed as

I realized, none of it was real. The ego is an empty illusion, caught in the trap of encapsulating itself within the body, which is an organism that dies. Everything seemed for a moment a huge cosmic joke. The universe was laughing compassionately at the amazing irony of life it was creating, and we are left out of this incredible joy and we have chosen to be. We continue to choose in blindness, slaves to our very own ego, which is nothing. I laughed so hard tears rolled down my cheeks, splashing and exploding with insight into reality. As the laughter calmed, I continued to experience Mother energy, but this time all mothers were connected to the Great Mother, Gaia, the creative, loving force of our world, and I was one with the beating heart of our planet, the beautiful living organism that is our home. The preciousness and gift of the Earth was over-whelming, and I saw how we take it for granted, pollute and destroy it without thought, and I saw the beauty of our attempts to care and love the planet and its gratitude for our kindness.

I continued to revel in ecstatic revelation. I understood how we forget, and I knew why and I knew I would again, but it was all so scrumptious, delicious and gorgeous. What we imagine as suffering and pain is a blessing for us to create, to know ourselves and create again in unique and extraordinary ways, continually expanding the creative force of Spirit.

I remained in this state for most of the day, and as evening began to dawn, I began to experience Julie again, but everything was new. I had been reborn and the exquisite delights that were waiting for me took me again into ecstasy unimagined before.

Sam was making himself an evening meal. I was incapable of performing any given task, as every step was new and beau-tiful. The wonder of walking was amazing, movement was a floating dance through the honeycomb of my home. The newness of the setting sun was almost too much to bear as I experienced the colors like never before. I felt them move through me, becoming orange and red ocean clouds swimming over the vast ocean below, with soft wind caressing me lightly as my colors deepened and vanished over the darkening water. It took me a good two hours to get up the stairs, and when I eventually ventured into the kitchen, I watched Sam take a bite of food. Astonishingly, I experienced the delights in my own body. This was extraordinarily marvelous. Sam encouraged me to eat myself, and as I put a cool red grape into my mouth, waves of orgasms flooded my body, and again I was on the floor, squealing with joy, discovering immeasurable pleasure of the senses. I was a flower with a thousand petals sharing my pollen with golden bees, sweet and pure. Oh, the wonderful joy of it all. And so it continued, way into the night until eventually, I crumbled in bed, my body exhausted, and I fell into a deep slumber.

On waking in the morning, I had returned, with all my boundaries and limitations, yet I had changed. I knew without a doubt, for I had experienced it, that we are all God consciousness, we are all one. That this journey of life is exquisite; boundaries are a necessary illusion so we can experience being human. And what struck me the most about this profound experience, was the experience of God-consciousness being ecstatic as it realized I was realizing I was God-consciousness. This creative force was as excited as "I" in my realization, for we are one, and we were united for a while in harmony and bliss. I felt God's joy in my moments of joy, the same. I know this is difficult to digest, and unless one has experienced this kind of phenomenon, it remains an enigma and an extraordinary tale. But it is indeed genuine. It is reality.

It can be easy to forget the truth, and be lulled and seduced into the drama of life. Emotion takes over and I do what I would rather not be doing, yet I have an understanding as I grow, that all the choices are mine as to how I handle my life. It is easier now to watch and see how I respond or react to situations. I almost hear my Soul wondering. "Is she going to shout or be calm, upset or understanding, stormy waters or peace?" And none of it really matters, and yet it does, for we can create peace within ourselves that will resonate outward to the world, and it feels like it is time for the world to experience peace and harmony. If we all reach this place inside ourselves, then that will be how the world is, for we are one. Mahatama Gandhi's words come to mind, *"The only devils in the world are those running in our own hearts. That is where the battle should be fought."*

A year later, after this joyous experience, I awakened again, in a new and unexpected way. For a moment, I realized myself again in exquisite moments of "Sat-Chit-Ananda," "being-consciousness-bliss." The ultimate reality.

"We don't receive wisdom," Marcel Proust said. *"We must discover it for ourselves after a journey that no one can take for us or spare us."*

My body twisted and contorted, I was moved as if I were a rag doll. I was aware I was moving into yoga positions I could have only dreamt about. Later I understood where yoga, meaning "union," originated and the purpose of the practice. My personal practice would evolve profoundly as a result. Yet I had not been practicing yoga postures, but had been sitting in quiet meditation observing my breath move through me in gentle waves, when by some unexpected force I was propelled into a non-ordinary state and a journey of Self-realization. It was the great emergence of energy that moved my body like a snake. Passionately opening the energy pathways and centers, allowing and demanding absolute freedom of movement, the energy spiraled upward. It was not my brain or my thinking mind that moved me, but pure cosmic energy, purging and purifying my body, tossing and turning me, stretching and shaking me to my core until one final thrust threw me from the wheel position onto my belly. With my chest, neck, arms and legs reaching backward and upward toward the sky, fierce heat streamed unmercifully, yet gloriously, through me. In the stillness of the intense position my breathing was heavy and heartbeat racing. Great cosmic bubbles of joy and excitement began to well in my lower belly. I could hear dramatic moans coming from me as the awesome feeling grew and multiplied. The brilliant bubbles turned to rapture and moved upward exploding spectacularly in the region of my heart. I was thrust wildly into a huge cosmic orgasm. Over and over again the bubbles exploded, filling every cell of my being with ecstasy and euphoria. Finally any notion of a separate self disappeared, shattered by bliss and divine luminosity and there was only Oneness. One Spirit realizing itself in exquisite love of a magnitude unbeknownst but to those who awaken to its glory. Oneness, and that is all.

And so how do I contain and integrate such experiences as I go on in my daily life? I have to realize that in this life we are separate; we create separateness so we can experience uniqueness, and free will. This is our reality for the time being. The journey of our consciousness is to evolve, until it all realizes itself again, merging euphorically with itself.

The greatest revelation to me is that enlightenment always exist within us, waiting for us to awaken. Through all the aspects of the ego, persona and shadow, the truth never strays. There is no goal to attain. We are already there, and we are all one, never truly separated beyond our limits of the human senses. The journey is to awaken this insight, to our God-self, and to our essence; to remerge with Self. As I move forward in life, I experience the illusion of pain, suffering, sadness. It does feel real now, for it is part of being human. But I know these are not who I am. I strive to hold these experiences while staying in my center, being balanced, bringing a sense of harmony to it all, and at some level really love it by being present to it, not allowing it to live me. This way I can make choices that create more joy, love and happiness for myself and others in this magical journey of life and death.

"My child, because you think you are the body, for a long time you have been bound. Know you are pure awareness. With this knowledge as your sword, cut through your chains and be happy!"
–Ashtavakra Gita

The intellectual conceptualization of the world not really existing, that everything is a dream, everything is energy and nothing really exists, intrigued and drew me. I contemplated this deeply. The illusion of life itself became clearer to explain in a deep meditation, exploring the Buddhist concepts of emptiness. I left my deep concentration of the breath for a few moments and searched for myself. Feeling my body buoyant and light, I searched intricately through it. But I did not exist in my physical structure, not even in my heart or my head. So where was I? Who was I? Is the self, then, an illusion of my own creation? I moved into the field of awareness that was aware of me searching for myself. This part that witnesses must be who I am, the sense of self, then, only a representation of my mind. Back to the breath which still existed as I expanded outward into an inner vastness, that which had been observing me. Not actively trying to bring anything about, just allowing the unfolding of what was to come or not, I kept my thoughts at bay. I had a powerful inner tool to assist me, a glowing sword of wisdom that recognized when a thought was about to emerge, and cut it off like a great warrior defending sacred territory. The outer environmental sounds began to change. A bird's song filtered into me as vibration, a wave of movement. A passing car was almost indistinguishable; like dust particles, its sound danced in the spaciousness that I was becoming. The sound of the ocean was in fact nothing but an internal creation of mind. Solidity of everything I was aware of dissolved, my perception altered, experienced from a new perspective of a larger mind, everything simply arising and passing away. My body was nothing but energy, floating somewhere in the vastness of who I am until it dissolved and left nothing but breath and space. For eternal moments the breath itself ceased; complete stillness, I was a void of no distinguishable character, in the timeless non-cognitive state of emptiness. Breath began again, each moment of it ageless. It became waves of expansion and contraction, small ripples arising and falling in the oceanic space and then experienced as tiny particles moving on an ocean wave. Inhalation, exhalation, arising and falling, until it was not arising and falling but one continuous stream of movement, the timeless continuum of breath movement, existing and yet not. The movement of wind blowing in no direction. There was only pure awareness of this awesome and vast spaciousness where time had ceased, and everything was experienced only as molecules of movement of expansion and contraction or vibration. But something shifted and I experienced a slight fear that sneaked in past the great sword.

My meditation came back into awareness. What was that? What was I about to experience? Something new, and yet almost too much to know. I was on a delicate precipice like none experienced before. "Do not limit yourself. Keep going and do not get attached, not even to the awesomeness," my mind intervened silently, slight whispers of my teacher guiding me gently back. I moved back into the awareness of emptiness and then it happened, or did not happen. The opulent intensity of something was close to me and began to envelope the vast awareness that I am, and I became, pure Cosmic Consciousness. Without beginning, without end, not even One.

Only moments, but they were timeless, infinite. A grand taste illuminated my mind to knowing that this is what is. Beyond the oneness of form, I experienced another taste of nirvana. In reflection, another moment to recognize the paradox. I am immeasurable and unbounded, and everything is created from emptiness, which is full.

My insights from this! Pure Cosmic Consciousness, not even One, all that is, without beginning nor end, formless, infinite, eternal. This is what we are. If I looked for our existence, our planet or even our universe in this, there is but a movement, a wave of some kind of energy that rippled, as tiny as a seed, in this non-place of no beginning and no end.

Of all of my experiences this shook me the most. I experienced a somber mood, a teariness that was haunting as I knew the illusion, and I could not be what I was any longer, yet nothing had changed. I did not dissolve into and become the space forever, and I wanted too.

"Okay," I screamed, "I'm ready to go now."

The world looked like a cruel joke for a while, and my only place of solace was within, yet an inner pain stirred. But in the quiet I saw the avenue of our mind as a place for God's expression, a place for the manifestation of the divine. I saw my place in the world as a conduit of awareness, with openness to continuing evolvement and to share my learning's with others as I learn from them. My capacity for compassion expanded greatly as I saw this in all of us. The power and potential of my experience influences how I walk my life, and it is with an open heart that I share what I know, knowing it is for us all.

None of this is new, of course. It has been written about beautifully through the ages. But this is my experience, the playing of my dream, and the sharing of my story so far.

"Nothing is like it seems, but everything is exactly like it is."
–Yogi Berra

About the Author

Julie Yau was born in England, and has lived mostly in the United States since she was seventeen.

With a background in performing arts, Julie changed her career after many non-ordinary experiences. Greatly inspired, she embarked on a transformative and illuminating journey of the exploration of body, mind and soul.

With an innate love of nature, she has traveled around the world, hiking mountains and exploring different cultures and countries including India, Tibet, Bhutan and Peru, while experiencing profound insights through meditation as well as spontaneous openings to non-ordinary states of consciousness.

Julie continues to devote herself to the exploration of consciousness, integrating and assimilating all that she learns, while sharing it with others.

Julie teaches yoga and meditation, as well as workshops with her husband, which incorporate a deep awareness of our wholeness and interconnectedness with others, embracing the mystery of being.

For more information visit the website:

julie@julieyau.com